Historic
American
Church and Social
Cookbooks

⎯⎯⬥⎯⎯

*Pages from classic cookbooks of the late nineteenth
and early twentieth centuries,
annotated and with updated recipes*

Edited by

Paul Schwartz
Lauri Shaw

&

AMPERSAND

Library of Congress Cataloging-in-Publication Data is available.

ISBN 978-0-9855681-3-9

Printed in the United States of America

10 9 8 7 6 5 4 3 2 1

Historic
American
Church and Social
Cookbooks

Contents

———◆———

Preface   vii

Choice Recipes (1922)   1

Club House Cook Book (1916)   15

Club House Cook Book (1904)   28

Favorite Recipes (1923)   40

Good Recipes (1906)   57

How We Cook in Los Angeles (1894)   71

My Mother's Cook Book (1880)   89

Fish, Flesh and Fowl (1894)   103

Hawaiian Cook Book (1920)   119

The Baptist Cook Book (1907)   135

Westminster Church Cook Book (1916)   148

The Housekeeper's Friend (1876)   158

Christianity in the Kitchen (1858)   174

Putting It All Together   184

Glossary   192

Preface

———◆———

There was one place in nineteenth- and early twentieth-century America where women were indisputably in charge and enjoyed free range of expression—the kitchen. For them, the home and the kitchen at its center were sources of power. One only has to read the cookbooks of the era to see this.

More than that, these women understood that homemaking and cooking could be used to make a moral statement in an age that was preoccupied with morality. The Foreword to *Favorite Recipes* (1923) states that cooking is "a very necessary incidental in the great work of building real character and life. . . . In our pursuit of great truths, of spiritual dynamic, and of nobler service to our fellow-men, we are not forgetful of those things which give us finer social qualities and breadth of intellectual grasp."

As to "breadth of intellectual grasp," these women were erudite. The books are peppered with quotes from the classics, Shakespeare, and contemporaries such as Ruskin. The writing is always beautiful; there is poetry in these pages.

The pages reproduced herein may be yellowed, foxed, stained with gravy, and marked with pencilled notes; the authors and their social groups long gone; the dishes quaint (but so intriguing); and the measures and directions sometimes unintelligible; but they give us an invaluable look into American kitchens and domestic life of a century and more ago.

Even if you do not cook, we hope you will find these pages as fascinating and entertaining as we do. We welcome your comments and suggestions for future volumes, and if you have a treasured antique cookbook that you would like to have reproduced in a future volume, please send it to us. We will guard it with our lives, return it in perfect condition, and give you a well-deserved credit. E-mail the editors at psampersand@yahoo.com.

Choice Recipes

(1922)

Choice Recipes was published in 1922 by the Order of the Eastern Star, a Masonic women's organization in Sacramento, California, to raise funds for the construction of Sacramento's Eastern Star Hall, which was built in 1928.

The hall is one of only four buildings constructed for the Eastern Star organization and the only one still surviving and in ac-

tive use. The building was listed in the National Register of Historic Places as a fine example of Romanesque Revival architecture, and a rare example of local buildings devoted to a women's organization.

The building was designed by the architectural firm of Coffman, Salsbury & Stafford in the Romanesque Revival style. An architect's drawing of the building includes five people in front of the building, all women. The women in the sketch were dressed in contemporary 1920s fashions, with bobbed hair and knee-length skirts, and one was behind the wheel of an automobile. This sketch provides insight into the changing role of women in the 1920s, and reflects the intended purpose of the building as the home of a women's organization. The building was completed in 1928, and used for both public and private functions. Many local schools used the hall's grand ballroom for dances and social functions. A fire in December 1936 temporarily closed the hall, but it was quickly repaired and reopened. Located directly across from the reconstructed Sutter's Fort, the hall became one of many social institutions around the Fort's perimeter on the eastern end of K Street.

CHOICE RECIPES

Edited and Compiled by

Members of the Eastern Star
of Sacramento

Add to your meal some merriment
  And a thought for kith and kin,
And then as a prime ingredient
  A plenty of wit thrown in.
But spice it all with the essence of love,
  And a litte whif of play,
Let a wise old book and a glance above
  Complete a well-spent day.

For the Benefit of the
Building Fund
Eastern Star Hall Association
of Sacramento, Cal.

FAVORITE RECIPES

of

Past Grand Matrons and Past Grand Patrons O. E. S. of California

ARTICHOKE RING
(Zelia Whitford Samson, W. G. M.)

Twelve artichokes
One cup cream
One cup milk
Six eggs
One cup bread crumbs (fresh).

Boil artichokes until they can be rubbed through a colander. Add cream, milk, bread crumbs, and well-beaten yolks of eggs, and when mixed fold in the stiffly-beaten whites. Pour in greased ring, set in pan of hot water, and bake in moderate oven until firm.

Filling

One pound sweetbreads
Two calves' brains
One can button mushrooms
One pint cream
Four tablespoons butter
Four tablespoons flour.

To the melted butter, add flour and cook until foamy, add cream, stir until thick and creamy, add salt; add mushrooms and blanched sweetbreads and brains, cut in dice.

To blanch sweetbreads and brains, soak one hour in cold water, drain, cover with cold water, add one tablespoon lemon juice or vinegar, two or three cloves, dash of pepper, and a tiny piece of bay leaf, simmer about fifteen minutes; drain and remove fibers.

SPICE CAKE
(Maud E. Bowes, P. G. M.)

One cup light brown sugar
One-half cup white sugar
Two eggs
One-half cup butter
Two-thirds cup milk
Three teaspoons baking powder
Two cups flour
One teaspoon each cinnamon and nutmeg
One-half teaspoon cloves

Cream butter and sugar. Add egg yolks, well beaten, sift together flour, baking powder and spices and add alternately with the milk. Fold in the beaten egg whites and add one teaspoon lemon juice. Bake in flat pan in moderate oven.

PRUNE CAKE
(Maud Dezell Bradley, P. G. M.)

One large cup prunes (cooked and cut up in small pieces)
One cup walnuts (cut with sharp knife)
One cup sugar
One cup butter
One and one-half cups flour
One teaspoon soda
One teaspoon baking powder
Six tablespoons sour milk
One-fourth teaspoon salt
One teaspoon cinnamon
One-half teaspoon cloves
One-half teaspoon nutmeg
One teaspoon lemon extract
One whole egg
Two yolks.

Cream butter and sugar. Add prunes, eggs well beaten, milk, flour, spices, walnuts, and last the soda and baking powder. Bake in three layers (moderate oven). Put together with boiled icing.

GINGERBREAD
(My Mother's Recipe)
(Guy Woodham Brundage, P. G. P.)

One-half cup sugar, one-half cup molasses, tablespoon shortening, mix thoroughly. Add one teaspoon soda, one teaspoon baking powder, two cups flour, one cup milk (sweet or sour), one-fourth teaspoon ginger, one-fourth teaspoon of cinnamon. Cook until done.

MRS. BYCE'S PLUM PUDDING
(Lyman C. Byce, P. G. P.)

Two lbs. currants
Two lbs. raisins
One lb. suet
Three-fourths lb. brown sugar
One lb. flour (sifted)
One-half lb. chopped citron and lemon peel together

One-half lb. fine bread crumbs
One large cup molasses
One tablespoon salt
One teaspoon cinnamon
One-half teaspoon cloves
One-half teaspoon nutmeg
Two tablespoons baking powder (Royal)
One cup blanched almonds (chopped)
Eight eggs, beaten good
Juice of one lemon
Two large cooking spoons extract of rose.

Mixing Order: Flour, sugar, spice, molasses, eggs, nuts, suet, lemon, raisins and currants. Last add baking powder. Mix well. If not moist enough add sweet milk.

Grease steeple mold well, and steam ten hours if all is for one pudding. When cooked in small cans, divide time according. Serve with hard sauce or cream.

BAKED FISH
(Benj. B. Cartwright, P. G. P.)

A fish weighing from four to six lbs. is a good size, and should be cooked whole. Make a stuffing of bread crumbs, butter, salt, pepper, a little salt pork, chop fine parsley and a little onion; mix in one egg; thoroughly fill the body of fish and sew it up; lay in a large dripping pan and lay across the top three or four strips of salt pork; put a pint of water in the pan and bake one and one-half hours; baste often. Serve with the following sauce: One cup vinegar; beat yolks of two eggs with tablespoon salad oil and two tablespoons prepared French mustard and a little red pepper; then add vinegar, a little at a time; beat well together.

PUMPKIN PUDDING
(Ernest W. Conant, P. G. P.)

One cup cooked and sifted pumpkin
One-half cup bread crumbs
One-half cup sugar, beaten with yolks of two eggs
One-half cup raisins
One-half teaspoon cinnamon
One-half teaspoon nutmeg
One-half teaspoon ginger
One cup rich milk.

Blend well, and bake in quick oven forty-five minutes. Cover with meringue made with whites of two eggs, one-half cup sugar and tablespoon ground nuts. Return to oven until a delicate brown.

PENOCHE
(A large recipe)
(W. K. Chambers, P. G. P.)

Three cups light brown sugar
One cup white sugar
Level teaspoon salt
One can Eagle Brand milk (Bordens, the kind babies use)
One cup water.

Put in kettle, stir all the time while cooking as it sticks if you do not. When soft ball stage, remove and set pan in basin of cold water. Add two tablespoons butter and one tablespoon vanilla, add walnuts, pour into buttered pan, mark off in squares. This is better next day.

ALMOND TORTE
(Chlo A. Craig, P. G. M.)

Three cups ground almonds
Six eggs
Two teaspoons of baking powder
One cup sugar
One tablespoon flour

Beat yolks of eggs and sugar, add ground almonds, flour and baking powder and the beaten whites of eggs. Bake in three layers and put together with whipped cream.

Almonds are not blanched.

PINEAPPLE-PEACH SALAD
(Ada Marsh Dalton, P. G. M.)

On crisp lettuce leaf lay one slice of pineapple. Fill center with freshly grated cheese, invert a half of canned peach over cheese, cover with mayonnaise to which has been added five tablespoons of whipped cream, and sugar to taste. Sprinkle top with chopped nuts and garnish with marischino cherry.

BEE HIVES
(Anna D. Dudderar, P. G. M.)

Line custard cups with spaghetti. (Take the long spaghetti and cook until tender, leave in water until lining the cups.) Fill cups with cheese souffle and bake twenty minutes. (Set cups in cold water when setting in oven.)

Cheese Souffle
(Anna D. Dudderar, P. G. M.)

Two tablespoons butter, three tablespoons flour, blend, and add one-half cup scalded milk, one-half teaspoon salt and a dash of cayenne, then one-fourth cup grated old English cheese or young American cheese. Remove from fire and add the yolks of three eggs beaten until lemon color. Cool mixture and fold in the whites of eggs beaten until stiff and dry. Pour in spaghetti lined custard cups and bake twenty minutes in a slow oven. Serve with creamed shrimp or crab.

SAUTE ROYAL (ENTREE)
(Mrs. P. W. Dohrmann, P. G. M.)

One medium lobster
One crab
One cup picked shrimps and fifty California oysters in their liquor.

Cut up six ripe tomatoes, one clove garlic, one large sweet pepper, one stalk celery and some parsley. Cook these together three-fourths of an hour, strain and set aside.

In another saucepan cook together one-half cup butter, one-half cup pastry cream and three tablespoons flour. When well blended add the oyster liquor, a wine glass sherry, a dash paprika and pinch of salt, and then the strained tomato sauce.

Now add the lobster, cut in dice; the shredded crab and the oysters, and cook until oysters curl on edge.

Serve hot in entree dishes with cheese-sticks.

Also delicious if made of sweetbreads and mushrooms substituted for lobster, etc.

ORANGE MARMALADE
(Effie Easton, P. G. M.)

One orange
One lemon
One grapefruit
Four pints of water
Four pounds of granulated sugar.

Fruit should be large and perfect as rinds are used. Wash fruit well, scrubbing with brush, dry thoroughly. Slice fruit without peeling thin and small. Remove seeds. Put sliced fruit into kettle with four pints of water, soak over night. In morning boil one and one-half hours (will be soft), add four pounds of sugar, boil for another one-half hour. Skim off surface impurities. Turn into glasses. When cold cover with melted paraffin, when hardened cover with the top.

This recipe will make ten glasses of A No. 1 marmalade.

BAKED STEAK
(Robert Edgar, P. G. P.)

Take a thick porterhouse or tenderloin steak, at least one inch thick; place in double roaster, cover with sliced onions and mushrooms, and over all pour a generous allowance of tomato catsup. Put a little water, season with salt and pepper, and bake in rather a slow oven for about one hour. Serve at once.

APPLE CAKE
(Louise Mae Elsensohn, P. G. M.)

One cup apples ground
One-half cup butter .
One cup sugar
One cup Sun-Maid raisins
Five tablespoons water
One teaspoon allspice
One teaspoon soda
One-half cup nut meats
Few grains salt
Flour.

Put apples through food grinder; cream butter and sugar; add ground apples, mix; add water, mix; add spices, salt and soda, mix; add fruit and nuts, mix; then stir into mixture flour enough to make very stiff. Bake one hour in slow oven.

WORLD'S FAIR CAKE
(Gertrude S. Freeman, P. G. M.)

Six tablespoons of grated chocolate, three of milk, three of sugar, put in a dish and beat till thoroughly dissolved. Three eggs beaten separately. One and one-half cups sugar, one-half cup butter creamed together; two cups flour with one teaspoon baking powder, one-half cup milk, add chocolate, yolks of eggs, half of the milk and flour to half of the creamed butter and sugar; the rest of the mixture with the white of eggs. Bake in two layers.

Frosting
Two cups sugar, one-half cup milk, butter size of an egg; boil ten or twelve minutes; beat till cold.

DEVIL CAKE
(Clara A. Giberson, P. G. M.)

One-half cup boiling water, one-half cup ground chocolate and one-half teaspoon soda; set aside to cool. One and one-half cups brown sugar, one-half cup butter; cream together. Add two well beaten eggs, one-half cup sour milk, pinch of salt, two cups flour, one teaspoon baking powder, rounded; mix well. Add cool mixture last. Bake in three layers. Sweet milk may be used, in which case, use two teaspoons baking powder; but add a pinch of soda to the first mixture, on account the brown sugar and chocolate.

Canapes

CANAPES SOUVAROFF

Prepare canapes of toast, lightly buttered; then spread one teaspoon of caviar on each. Finely chop the white of hard-boiled egg, evenly sprinkle over canapes; then arrange an anchovy in oil, ring shape, on center of each and fill the inside of anchovy with a little chopped parsley. Decorate dish with parsley and lemon and serve.

CANAPES DANOIS

Prepare six medium-sized bread canapes, two and one-half inches in diameter. Cover each with a very thin slice of cooked ham, the same size as the bread. Spread a little French mustard over the ham. Cut six very thin slices of smoked salmon, the size of the ham. Cut in half and arrange on top of half the ham; spread one-half teaspoon of caviar over other half of ham. Hash very finely one cold hard-boiled egg and sprinkle over canapes evenly. Decorate dish with lemon and parsley and serve.

CANAPES WITH ARTICHOKES

Cook artichokes, remove leaves and fuzzy centers; place on pieces of toast, lightly buttered; spread with anchovy paste. Decorate with pickled cucumbers, capers or gherkins and hard-boiled eggs, finely chopped. Dot with mayonnaise and sprinkle with paprika.

CANAPES, MORENO-RUSSE

Prepare toast canapes and spread a teaspoon caviar on top of each. Chop very fine sweet Spanish red pepper and evenly spread over caviar. Dress dish with small pieces of lettuce and serve.

CRAB MEAT CANAPE

Mix together one-half cup Namco crab meat, chopped; one-fourth cup mayonnaise dressing; one teaspoon anchovy paste; two olives, finely chopped. Spread on pieces of toast cut in two-inch diamonds. Garnish the edge with finely-chopped hard cooked egg, mixed with chopped parsley. Garnish the top with fine lines of butter, creamed, flavored highly with anchovy paste, and forced through a pastry bag and small rose tube. Serve as the first course at a formal dinner. Canapes may be covered with melted aspic jelly if they must stand some time before being served.

CANAPES

(Ethel S. Camtee)

Cut sliced bread into hearts, rounds or diamonds; fry light brown in butter.

(1) Spread lightly with mustard, then sprinkle with grated cheese; garnish with slices of stuffed olives.

(2) Mince crab or shrimps, mix with mayonnaise and spread on bread; garnish with green pepper.

(3) Bone and mash sardines, season with lemon juice and Worcestershire sauce; spread on bread; garnish with hard-boiled egg.

PEPPER CANAPES

(Sarah Eliza Hall, P. W. M., Honolulu)

Cut rounds of bread one-third inch thick from a stale loaf. Brown quickly in hot butter in a frying pan.

Mix together:

Two chopped hard-cooked eggs
Two tablespoons chopped pimentos
One-half teaspoon salt

Soups

CREOLE OYSTER GUMBO
One tablespoon Lea & Perrins Sauce
Two dozen oysters
One Spanish onion
Two tablespoons olive oil
One tablespoon flour
One teaspoon salt.

Drain the liquor from the oysters and save. Heat the oil and add the chopped onion. Add the flour and salt. Cook for a few minutes and add the oyster liquor and the oysters. Cook for five minutes longer. Add the Lea & Perrins Sauce and serve.

ALMOND SOUP
Ingredients:
One-fourth ℔. almonds
One teaspoon flour
Two hard-boiled eggs
One quart of stock, beef preferred
One cup cream or very rich milk
Salt and pepper.

Method: Put unblanched almonds in boiling water and let stand until skin becomes loose. Pour off water and remove the skins. Put the almonds through a food chopper. Mix with finely-chopped yolks of eggs and add to the stock and let come to a boil. Make a paste of the flour and a little cold water and add to the above. Add salt and pepper. Let simmer until ready to serve. Just before serving add cream or milk and the finely-chopped whites of eggs.

This soup is especially nice if each serving is garnished with a teaspoon of whipped cream.

CELERY SOUP
Two heads of celery
One quart of milk

One cup of rice
Veal or chicken broth
Pepper and salt.

Grate or cut fine the celery, and boil it in the milk with the rice very slowly until done. Add more milk if too thick; then add an equal quantity of veal or chicken broth; pepper and salt to taste. Serve very hot with toast cut in dice shape or strain and serve in bouillon cups, placing in each a ring of green peppers.

CHICKEN GUMBO
Put in a pot one tablespoon of sifted flour and the same of butter; let it become a rich brown; add one chicken cut up, and season with salt, pepper, onion and a little tomato. Pour into this two quarts of hot water, let boil two hours. Thirty minutes before serving, add one quart of oysters, one tablespoon of mashed bay leaves and one tablespoon of butter. Serve hot.

CONSOMME
Three pounds of soup beef
Three pounds of veal knuckle
Three and one-half quarts of water
Six slices of salt pork
One cupful each of chopped onion, celery, carrot
One bunch of parsley
One tablespoon of salt.

Cut the salt pork into fine pieces and brown. Add the veal, cut into pieces, add the beef and sear together with the salt pork. Add the water and any cracked bones and simmer for three hours. Add the vegetables and salt and cook an hour more. Set aside to cool, skim the fat from the top and strain the

Fish

BAKED FISH WITH CHEESE
(Mrs. F. A. Morrill)

One pound halibut
Four slices salt pork
One-half pound cheese
Salt and pepper.

Cut the salt pork in bits and put in an enamelware or aluminum baking pan; lay fish on top, dust with salt and pepper, cover with the cheese, which has been put through the coarse knife of the food chopper, and bake about twenty minutes in a hot oven. The fish should be cut about a half-inch thick.

BAKED FISH
(Mabel B. Seymour)

A fish weighing from four to six lbs. is a good size, and should be cooked whole. Make a stuffing of bread crumbs, butter, salt, pepper, a little salt pork, chop fine parsley and a little onion; mix in one egg; thoroughly fill the body of fish and sew it up; lay in a large dripping pan and lay across the top three or four strips of salt pork; put a pint of water in the pan and bake one and one-half hours; baste often.

Serve with the following sauce: One cup vinegar; beat yolks of two eggs with tablespoon salad oil and two tablespoons prepared French mustard and a little red pepper; then add vinegar, a little at a time; beat well together.

BAKED DEVILED CLAMS
(Mrs. Robert Edgar)

Two cups minced clams
One-half cup corn
One-half cup ground salt pork
One-half cup bread crumbs
Two tablespoons olive oil
One tablespoon Worcestershire sauce
One tablespoon onion and garlic juice
Add one beaten egg, and mix all together.

Season to taste with pepper, salt, sage, thyme and marjoram. Place in shells and bake one-half hour. Serve hot with grated cheese and cocktail sauce.

MOLDED CRAB SALAD

Soak two teaspoons gelatine in one-half cup chicken stock or water and dissolve over hot water. Add one tablespoon tarragon vinegar, then add slowly to one cup mayonnaise dressing, beating thoroughly. Pare a grape fruit, remove sections free from membrane and cut in pieces. To one-half cup pulp add one-half cup canned pineapple cut in small cubes, one small can crab meat, free from bones, and the gelatine mayonnaise. Pack in small molds and put in a cold place. When ready to serve, remove salad from molds and place in nests of lettuce leaves. Cover smoothly with mayonnaise dressing and garnish with a maraschino cherry on each salad. This is a nice salad for a party or a buffet spread.

CRAB COCKTAIL
(Serves 6)

One cup cream
One cup catsup
Four tablespoons lemon juice
Four tablespoons Worcestershire sauce
Salt, pepper
One picked crab.

Put catsup into cream, very little at a time—catsup in minority always.

CRAB CREOLE
(For 6)
(Mrs. Grace Hicks)

Two oz, butter
Three small onions
Two green peppers
Salt, red pepper
One tomato
One tablespoon flour
One-half cup cream.

Chop onions and peppers (without seeds) very fine and put in stew-pan with butter, salt and pepper. Stir slowly ten minutes and add tomato (peeled). Stir this until dissolved; add flour mixed with cream and make it thick as drawn butter; put in finely picked crab.

CRAB COCKTAIL
(Emma R. Leach)

Five heaping teaspoons stiff mayonnaise
Ten heaping tablespoons whipped cream
Six tablespoons Snyder's cocktail sauce
Two teaspoons Worcestershire sauce
One teaspoon catsup
One-half teaspoon salt
One pimento, cut into small pieces

Mix all together in a dish rubbed with garlic. Add the meat of two large or three small crabs. This will serve twelve

SCALLOPED TUNA
(Elizabeth Goshen)

Butter the sides and bottom of a deep baking dish. Begin with a ½-inch layer of fresh bread broken in small pieces, then a layer of fish picked into small bits. Sprinkle with salt, pepper and a little baking powder, and plenty of small pieces of butter. Then bread, fish, etc., as before until dish is full, with a last layer of bread on top. Pour boiling hot milk over until covered. Bake about one-half hour in slow oven, cover the first ten minutes.

One and one-half teapsoons baking powder

One pint milk

One can tuna.

MOCK CRABS
(Mrs. F. A. Morrill)

One-fourth cup butter

One-half cup flour

Three-fourths teaspoon mustard

One and one-half teaspoons salt

One-fourth teaspoon paprika

One and one-half cups milk

One can corn

One egg

Three teaspoons Worcestershire sauce

Melt the butter, add flour, mustard, salt, and paprika, and gradually the milk. Turn in the corn, add the eggs slightly beaten, and the Worcestershire sauce. Pour into a buttered fire-proof dish, cover with one cup cracker crumbs, mixed with two tablespoons melted butter, and bake till browned.

CREAMED CRAB WITH EGGS

Add to creamed crab meat three hard-cooked eggs cut in eighths and serve on toast with bacon curls.

SHRIMP WIGGLE

One cup shrimps

One cup canned peas

Four tablespoons butter

Three tablespoons flour

One-half tablespoon salt

One and one-half cups milk

One-fourth can pimento.

Make a white sauce, add to pimento, peas and shrimps, serve on crackers.

CREAMED LOBSTER IN PATTIES
(Mary B. Dixon, D. G. M.)

Two cups diced boiled lobster

One cup mushrooms, broken in pieces

One-half small onion, cut fine

One tablespoon green pepper, minced

One tablespoon parsley, minced

One tablespoon pimento, cut in small pieces

Three tablespoons butter

Two tablespoons flour

One-half teaspoon salt

Dash of cayenne

Dash of nutmeg

Two egg yolks, well beaten

One and three-fourths cups coffee cream, three fourths cup milk, making two and one-half cups.

Melt butter in double boiler, add onion, green pepper, parsley, pimento and mushrooms; stir and cook together for fifteen minutes. Add flour, mixing thoroughly, then add two cups of the milk and cream, reserving one-half cup; add lobster and cook ten minutes. Just before serving add the remaining one-half cup of milk to beaten yolks and pour into lobster; cook five minutes longer and serve immediately in pattie shells or on hot, buttered toast.

MUSSELS AND CLAMS
(Maud E. Gilpin)

Wash thoroughly, put a good-size piece of butter in a pot and melt, then put in the clams or mussels. Chop up parsley and a cone of garlic very fine, add salt and pepper to suit taste; cover up and let steam until they open.

OYSTER COCKTAILS
(For 6 persons)

One hundred oysters

Two limes (juice)

One tablespoon Worcestershire sauce

Six tablespoons tomato catsup

One tablespoon vinegar

Two teaspoons pepper

Salt, dash tabasco.

Select small California oysters, mix all together and serve.

DEVILED SARDINES
(Chafing Dish)

Two tablespoons oil (drained from sardines)

One-half tablespoon Worcestershire sauce

One-half tablespoon vinegar

One teaspoon lemon juice

One-fourth teaspoon salt

One-eighth teaspoon paprika.

Put sardines in chafing dish. Pour over above mixture and cook, turning frequently. Serve on wafers or toast.

SHRIMP SAVORY
(Dr. Lew Wallace, P. G. P.)

One tablespoon melted butter

One teaspoon chopped onion

One cup boiled rice

One cup shrimps

One cup cream

One teaspoon Worcestershire sauce

One-third cup tomato catsup

Pepper and salt to taste.

Mix all together and cook in a double boiler. This will serve six.

Entrees

BRAINS DEVILED

One teaspoon English mustard
Two teaspoons Parisian sauce
One-third teaspoon red pepper
One teaspoon salt.

Clean brains until white by picking off the skins in cold water. Mix mustard, Parisian sauce, red pepper and salt together. Into this mixture roll brains; then into bread crumbs and fry, until brown on both sides, in a frying pan. Over this pour enough water to make gravy, and boil about ten minutes. Thicken gravy to taste and serve hot.

BRAIN TIMBALES
(Maud E. Gilpin)

Two sets calves brains, two large slices of bread soaked in milk, four eggs, well beaten. Mix well and season with salt, pepper, a pinch of ginger, paprika and Worcestershire sauce. Steam three-quarters of an hour in well-buttered molds.

Sauce

One tablespoon butter, one tablespoon flour, one-half pint cream, salt, pepper, paprika, juice of one lemon and two tablespoons of catsup, one-half can mushrooms and one pinch of nutmeg.

Beat brains to a cream. Sqeeze bread dry and add to brains. Add well-beaten eggs. Grease molds well. Place in pan of water and bake three-quarters of an hour. Serve with cream tomato sauce.

CROQUETTES
(12 Croquettes)

Use white sauce. Set aside until thoroughly chilled. Mix in cubed meat or fish in equal quantity, one hard-boiled egg chopped coarsely, chopped parsely. Mold in croquette or cylinder shapes,

roll in bread crumbs, then in beaten egg, then bread crumbs again. Set aside for a few moments to dry. Fry in deep fat. Serve with a white sauce. Fat to be 240-260 degrees.

SURPRISE CROQUETTES

One cup of cold boiled ham pickings
One-half teaspoon of dry mustard
One-half teaspoon of dry sage
One quart of mashed potatoes
One egg
One cup of dry bread crumbs.

The potato should be one inch thick on a platter. Divide into eight parts and put a tablespoon of ham mixture, which has been put through a food chopper and mixed with the mustard and sage, on the center of each part. Cover with the potato, shape oblong and dip in bread crumbs, then in beaten egg, and then in bread crumbs again. Fry in deep hot fat. Drain on brown paper. Serve with parsley.

ANGELS ON HORSEBACK

Mix a little lemon juice, cayenne, essence of anchovy; then dip in mixture Eastern oysters and roll each one in thin slice of bacon. Put these so prepared oysters on a skewer and fry them in clarified butter; place each oyster on a piece of fresh-made toast and serve very hot.

CHEESE CROQUETTES
(Jennie E. Adams)

Two and one-half cups milk
One cup Germea
One egg yolk
One tablespoon Worcestershire sauce
Two teaspoons salt

One teaspoon dry mustard
One-fourth lb. grated cheese.

Boil milk, add Germea, and cook twenty minutes. Take from stove and add balance of ingredients. Mix thoroughly; cool, shape; roll in egg, then in crumbs, and fry in deep fat. Serve plain with parsley, with cream or tomato sauce.

CHEESE FONDU
(Stella Morgan Linscott)

Mix:
One cup milk
One cup bread crumbs (small)
One cup grated cheese.

Put into a double boiler over the fire. When the cheese is melted add:
One beaten egg
One tablespoon olive oil
One level teaspoon mustard
Salt and pepper to taste.

Cook till thick and serve on slices of buttered toast.

CHEESE SOUFFLE
(Jennie E. Adams)

Two tablespoons butter
One tablespoon flour
One-half cup hot milk
One teaspoon salt
One cup grated cheese
Three eggs (beaten separately)
Paprika to suit.

Melt butter; add flour, stir smooth; add milk and stir until thickened. Remove from stove. Add cheese, egg yolks well beaten, and fold in whites beaten stiff and dry. Bake thirty minutes in buttered dish. 250°.

CHEESE SOUFFLE WITH VARIATIONS

Heat milk in double boiler, add bread crumbs, let stand ten minutes. Beat egg yolks and add to milk, then butter, cheese, salt, fold in beaten whites, bake thirty minutes in slow oven. (If using only egg yolks use one-third of whites given in recipe and add one teaspoon baking powder.)

Use spinach in place of cheese, only one cup cooked and chopped fine, or cheese and carrot (left over), or corn. Cut down on milk when using canned corn.

CREAMED SWEETBREADS
(Mabel B. Seymour)

Allow sweetbreads to stand in water to which has been added one teaspoon of salt, one or two hours before cooking. Boil until tender. Cover with cold water, allow to cool and pull apart removing membrane.

White Sauce

Two tablespoons flour
One tablespoon butter
One cup rich milk
One-half teaspoon salt
One-half teaspoon pepper.

Add sweetbreads to sauce, allow to cook until heated thoroughly. This may be served in ramekins or patty cases.

BRAISED SWEETBREADS
(Mabel B. Seymour)

Boil, after soaking in salt water, remove membrane and put in pan in oven with one tablespoon butter and when nicely brown, turn other side. Season with salt and pepper. Serve on toast.

ENTREE OF GIBLETS
(Mabel B. Seymour)

Cook thoroughly hearts, livers and gizzards of several chickens; chop rather fine; thicken the liquor; season highly, adding a few drops of burnt onion juice, lemon juice, some chopped mushrooms and a little of the liquor, as well as sherry, the quantities depending on the quantity of giblets; put all into buttered ramekins or individual baking dishes, put bread crumbs and bits of butter on top and bake for five or ten minutes. Chopped veal may be added to the giblets to increase the quantity.

LAMB TERRAPIN
(May P. Walters)

Cut cold lamb or veal in dice. Make sauce of one tablespoon butter, one-half tablespoon flour, one-half teaspoon mustard, one teaspoon currant jelly, one teaspoon Worcestershire sauce, paprika, salt.

Add one-half cup stock, little cream, yolks of two hard-boiled eggs (run through ricer). Beat all smooth, add meat, whipped whites, and tablespoon sherry. Serve on toast.

RED DEVIL

One can pimentos
One lb. cheese
One can tomato soup.

Melt cheese in double boiler. Heat soup and pour into melted cheese, stir constantly. Cut pimentos into small pieces, flavor with salt and paprika. Serve on toast or crackers.

CRAB MEAT A LA NEWBURG

Melt four tablespoons butter, add one large can crab meat from which bones have been removed and stir and cook three minutes, keeping pieces as large as possible. Sprinkle with three-fourths teaspoon salt, few grains cayenne, few grains nutmeg, two teaspoons lemon juice and one teaspoon Worcestershire sauce. Add one-half cup thin cream mixed with two egg yolks. Place over hot water and stir gently until thickened. Serve at once on half slices of toasted bread.

RICE AND CHEESE LOAF

To two and one-half cups of cooked rice, add one cup of grated American cheese, one minced green pepper, one and one-half teaspoons of salt, one-eighth teaspoon paprika and one egg, slightly beaten. Put in a well-oiled loaf pan and bake at 500° Fahrenheit for twenty-five minutes. Serve hot, with a sauce made by heating one can of tomato soup.

SHRIMP TARDO

One can shrimps
One cup rice (cooked)
One cup thick cream
One tablespoon melted butter
One tablespoon grated onion
Three-fourths tablespoon Worcestershire sauce
One-third cup tomato catsup.

Melt butter, fry onion, add shrimps, rice, then sauce and catsup. Bake twenty minutes.

CRAB MEAT CROUSTADES
(Mrs. Grace Hicks)

Cut stale bread in slices two inches thick and shape in diamonds, squares or circles. Remove centers leaving cases with walls one-third inch thick. Brush with melted butter and brown delicately in hot oven or under gas flame. Fill with Crab Meat a la King or Crab Meat a la Newburg or Creamed Crab Meat. Garnish with parsley.

COOKING CEREAL

If cereal is started the night before it is to be used, prevent a crust from forming over the top by putting a cup of cold water over the top after the cereal has stopped cooking. In the morning pour the water off and heat the cereal.

TAMALE LOAF

(Elizabeth B. Wheeler, P. G. M.)

One can tomatoes
One can corn
Two cups olive oil
One-fourth cup butter
One cup chipped chicken
One teaspoon salt
Two onions
Three cloves garlic
Pepper

Several chile tepins (they are nice and hot).
Cook until done, then let cool, then add:
Three eggs, well beaten
One cup milk
Two cups yellow corn meal
Season with cayenne pepper and chili powder.
Bake thirty-five minutes.

Updated Version

Ingredients:
1 lb. ground turkey
1 red bell pepper and 1 orange bell pepper, chopped
1 onion, chopped
3 cloves of garlic, minced
1 14.5 oz. can of creamed corn
1 14.5 oz. can of diced tomatoes
1 cup of yellow cornmeal
1 small can of sliced black olives, drained
2 eggs
1 tablespoon chili powder
2 teaspoons salt
A pinch of pepper
Salsa, optional

Directions:
Preheat oven to 350 degrees. In a large skillet, cook the ground turkey, peppers, onion, and garlic, until the meat is no longer pink. Drain when finished cooking. In a separate pot, cook the corn, tomatoes, and cornmeal for 10 minutes on low, stirring well. Remove from heat and mix in the eggs and olives. Pour the corn mixture over the ground beef and vegetables and mix well, then pour into a greased 9 x 12 pan. Bake uncovered for 1 hour. Top with salsa, if desired.

Club House Cook Book

(1916)

The *Club House Cook Book* was published by the Woman's Club of Reading, Pennsylvania, in 1916. Sales of the book raised funds that enabled the club to move into the former Wyomissing Club building, which dates from the late nineteenth century. The building, located at 140 North Fifth Street in the historic heart of downtown Reading, contains a 265 seat auditorium renowned for its perfect acoustics and is now the home of the Woman's Club of Reading (WCR) Center for the Arts.

CLUB HOUSE

COOK BOOK

Compiled by

ANNIE IAEGER SNYDER (MRS. JEFFERSON)

OF THE WOMAN'S CLUB OF READING, PA., DURING THE SUMMER
OF 1916, TO BE SOLD FOR THE BENEFIT OF THE CLUB HOUSE
FUND OF THE WOMAN'S CLUB OF READING, PENNSYLVANIA.

COMMITTEE ON CLUB HOUSE FUND

BELLE L. EBUR, Chairman

HANNAH COTTEREL	HATTIE KLAPP ROTHERMEL
ANNIE K. EBUR	LILLIE C. POMEROY
ADELAIDE K. HENDEL	EMMA HENDEL SPANG
MARY BAER HIESTER	MARY ELIZABETH ULRICH
M. LOUISE HILL	MARY ALICE WEAND
MABEL C. L. JONES	ADELAIDE WRIGHT
SARAH D. KEELY	BLANCHE AUGUSTA ZIEBER
EMILY BAER KNAPP	ANNIE IAEGER SNYDER

Escolloped Eggs and Oysters—Melt some butter, season with salt, pepper, a pinch of grated nutmeg, chopped parsley and chives. Cook 4 dozen oysters in this sauce and when nearly done, add 5 or 6 sliced hard boiled eggs. Simmer over a slow fire for ¼ of an hour. Pour in scollop shells, sprinkle with grated bread crust and brown in oven.

Escolloped Oysters—To 50 oysters (a salt oyster being the best) take 4 hard boiled eggs chopped fine, ¼ pound butter, two or 3 cups of fine bread crumbs. Divide the oysters, eggs and bread crumbs into two parts. Put ½ the oysters into a buttered pudding dish, season with salt and pepper and a pinch of cayenne, then put a layer of ½ of the chopped eggs and dots of ½ the butter, then a layer of ½ the bread crumbs; make the next layer just the same way, but cover thickly on top with bread crumbs and dots of butter. Pour in a little milk and bake in oven about an hour.

ANNIE SNYDER.

Clams in Casserole—One dozen clams put through the meat grinder, 2 eggs, 1 cup bread crumbs, ½ cup cream, 2 tablespoonfuls melted butter, mince onion, parsley, salt and pepper to taste.   INEZ RASHBRIDE.

Salmon Loaf—One can of salmon, 4 tablespoonfuls melted butter, ½ cup fine bread crumbs, 3 eggs beaten light, juice of 1 lemon, seasoning. Steam 1 hour and brown. Serve with cream sauce or cold with lettuce or mayonnaise.

ANNA L. HUFFORD.

Fricassee of Oysters—Drain one quart of oysters and put the liquor on to boil. Rub together one tablespoonful of butter and one of flour, add to the boiling liquor and stir it until it thickens. Season with salt, a very little cayenne pepper and a blade of mace. Remove it from the fire and add the beaten yolks of two eggs. Mix thoroughly and return to the fire, stirring for a minute or two. Put in the oysters and boil up again. Pour over slices of buttered toast and serve.

SWEET BREADS

"Variety's the very spice of life
That gives it all its flavor."—Cowper.

Sweet Bread Patties With Oysters and Mushrooms—
One-half pound of sweet-breads, 2 dozen oysters, 1 can or ¼ pound fresh mushrooms, 3 hard boiled eggs, ½ cup of chopped celery, 1 tablespoon minced parsley, ½ pint of cream, ½ pint of milk, 1 tablespoonful of butter, 1 tablespoonful of flour, salt and cayenne to taste. Boil sweet breads 20 minutes in salt water, blanch and remove all skin, break into small pieces. Heat oysters in own liquor, until edges curl, strain. Heat cream and milk. Rub together flour, butter and seasoning, and mix with hot cream and milk. Stir until it boils and is very smooth. Mix all together and fill shells. For 1 dozen patty shells.   MRS. IRVIN S. ERMENTROUT.

Fried Sweet-Breads—Trim and blanch your sweet breads, and dip them into luke warm stock to which you have added melted butter, chopped herbs, onion, the juice of a lemon, salt and pepper. Dip them into a batter and fry a golden brown. Serve with tomato sauce and garnish with mushrooms.

Lamb's Sweetbreads No. 1—Put them in hot water and simmer for a full half hour. Pour away all but ½ pint of water and let simmer 2½ or 3 hours, when nearly done add salt and pepper, ketchup and thicken with 1 tablespoon of flour mixed with 2 tablespoonfuls cold water. Let boil 2 minutes and serve.

Lamb's Sweetbreads No. 2—Two sweetbreads, 1 egg, breadcrumbs, ½ pint of gravy, 3 tablespoonfuls sherry. Soak sweetbreads in cold water for 1 hour, then put in boiling water to render firm. Stew gently for 15 minutes; take them out and drain in a cloth. Brush over with yolk of egg and bread crumbs, fry in hot lard until brown. Heat the gravy, season with pepper and salt. Add sherry, pour over the sweetbreads and serve.   FANNY BARON,
Chorley Wood, England.

Cream Mushroom Sauce (Croquettes, Fillet of Beef)— Melt 1 tablespoonful of butter without browning; add 1 table- spoonful of flour, stir until it is smooth; then add ½ cupful of cream and ½ cupful of mushroom liquor, salt and pepper to taste; cut ½ can of mushrooms with a silver knife, and add just before the same begins to thicken. They should only cook long enough to be heated through, and served at once.

MRS. A. S.

Celery Sauce—Wash and cut into inch pieces 1 medium sized stalk of celery, and boil until tender in milk and water; season with white pepper, nutmeg and salt, and thicken with a scant tablespoon of butter and flour rubbed together.

Caper Sauce—Mix ¼ pound of butter with the same quantity of flour, a tumblerful of water, salt and pepper in a saucepan. When boiling take off the fire, stir in ½ pound of butter; put some capers in a sauce boat and pour the sauce over them. Do not allow this sauce to become too thick, and make just before serving.

Curry Sauce—Take 3 ounces of butter and a dessert- spoonful of curry powder. Stir over the fire until the butter begins to melt. Moisten with strong stock or gravy, reduce, skim off all grease, and warm in a bain-marie. When ready to serve stir in a lump of butter and season a little more, if necessary.

Anchovy Sauce—Skin and scrape some well soaked an- chovies, pass through a tammy and stir in the same quantity of butter as there is paste.

Mint Sauce (Roast Lamb)—Reduce equal quantities of vinegar and water, sweeten with a lump of sugar and stir in some finely chopped mint.

Robert Sauce—Brown some slices of onion in butter and add a little flour, moisten with stock, white wine and a few drops of vinegar. Boil for ½ hour, skim off all grease, season with salt and pepper. Stir in a teaspoonful of mustard and serve.

POULTRY and GAME

Baked Squab—Draw, singe and truss, place in body 1 sprig of celery, 1 bay leaf, one small sprig of parsley, one small slice of onion and dust well, inside and out, with salt and pepper; pour over one tablespoon full of olive oil; place in pan ¼ cup of boiling water, put in quick oven and cook from ¾ to one hour, basting every 10 minutes.

Roast Turkey—Wash, singe and draw a young, plump turkey, rub it with salt and pepper inside and out, and stuff it with tender bread crumbs moistened only with melted butter or fat drawn from the fowl. The fat gives a better flavor and may be quickly melted. To a bowlful of crumbs add a teaspoonful of thyme, or sweet marjoram, or both, a saltspoon of pepper, a teaspoonful salt, and a little onion juice. Mix the filling well and after it has been pressed under the loose skin and into the body, skewer the fowl. Draw the legs firmly against the body, fold the wings under the back and tie all firmly together with plenty of clean cotton cord. Now grease the turkey well with butter, olive oil, or the like, dredge with flour and place it on a trivet in a hot oven to sear quickly that the juices will not escape during the roasting proper. When the skin is well seared, lessen the heat and baste the turkey frequently from a pint of hot water turned into the pan as soon as the flour on the turkey has been nicely browned. An 8 pound turkey should be allowed three hours in a moderate oven, and it may be dredged with flour a second time, about an hour before it is to be served. In the meantime boil the gibblets in a little salted water, and when done, chop fine and return to the water in which they were boiled. After the turkey has been lifted to the platter, turn the giblets and water into the roasting pan and let the gravy boil. The flour that has been basted from the turkey will usually make the gravy thick enough, but if this is insufficient, dredge browned flour into the pan until the gravy is creamy as it boils up. It will then be ready to serve. The roasting turkey will as a rule impart sufficient seasoning to the gravy, but more may be added, if necessary.

Corn Pudding No. 1—Scrape the substance out of fresh uncooked corn, add melted butter, pepper, salt and sugar to taste, add yolks and whites of 3 eggs beaten separately, 1 cup of milk mixed with the yolks. Put into a baking dish and bake ½ or ¾ of an hour. MRS. GEORGE D. HORST.

Corn Pudding No. 2—Twelve ears corn grated, 3 eggs beaten separately, 1 cup milk, 1 tablespoonful melted butter, 1 tablespoonful flour, pepper and salt. Bake in the oven ½ hour.   " NORRISTOWN."

Corn Pudding No. 3—One dozen large ears of corn, 1 pint of milk, 4 eggs, 1 teaspoonful salt, ¼ teaspoonfuls black pepper. Score the corn down the centre of each row of grains, then with the back of the knife, press out all the pulp, leaving the hull on the cob; beat the whites and yolks separately, add yolks to the corn, mix thoroughly, add salt, pepper and milk, and stir in the whites carefully. Put in a pudding dish. Bake slowly one hour. A tablespoonful of sugar is nice in corn pudding.   " NORRISTOWN."

Canned Corn Pudding—Mince corn, beat 3 eggs separately, add 1 tablespoonful of sugar, 2 tablespoonfuls melted butter, even teaspoonful salt, a cup of milk. Fold in whites of eggs. Bake in a greased pudding dish half hour, then uncover to brown slightly.

MRS. McCOY, York.

Creamed Cucumbers—Cut cucumbers lengthwise into several parts, boil 20 minutes or until tender. Serve like asparagus on buttered toast with cream dressing. Tender spring onions may be served the same way when boiled.

MRS. HARRY MAURER.

Sweet Potato and Marshmallow—Sweet potatoes, sugar, butter, salt and marshmallows. Boil potatoes in unsalted water, until tender; remove the skins and mash as Irish potatoes, stir into them sugar, butter and salt to taste. Place in a buttered baking dish, cover the top with marshmallows. Put in the oven until the mashmallows brown and swell.

NELLIE GERY.

German Shoo-Fly—Line 4 pie plates with rich pastry. Mix ½ cup of butter and lard, 3 cups of flour, 1 cup of brown sugar. Mix 1 cup of molasses (dark), 1 cup of boiling water, 1 scant, level tablespoon soda. Mix all together and sprinkle some of the crumbs on top, or put liquid into lined pans and sprinkle all of the crumbs on top. Spices can be added. MRS. GEORGE STRICKLER.

Why the Pie Boils Over—When the fruit in tarts boils over it is because the bottom heat is too strong, as is often the case in a gas stove. To prevent this, stand the pie dish in another containing water or on a tin covered with a little sand.

Lemon Custard—Make a pastry and bake it. Two cups of water, 2 cups of sugar, 1 lemon, 2 tablespoonfuls of corn starch and 3 eggs. S. M.

Doughnuts, Diamond Ponds—One cup of sugar, 1 egg and a little salt beaten together, 1 cup of sour milk, 1 tablespoonful of sour cream or 1 tablespoon of hot lard out of the frying dish, 1 teaspoonful of soda. Flour enough to roll out well. MRS. HERBERT LITTLE.

Crumb Cake—Mix thoroughly 2 cups of sugar, ¾ cups of butter and lard, 3¾ cups of flour, 2 teaspoonfuls baking powder, ½ grated nutmeg. Take out ½ of the crumbs to sprinkle on top, add 3 well beaten eggs and 1 cup of sweet milk. Divide into 4 pie plates, and sprinkle crumbs on top. Bake quickly. MRS. GEORGE STRICKLER.

Sweet or White Potato Pie—One and one-half pounds of potatoes, mashed, without milk, ½ pound of butter melted, 6 eggs, ¾ pounds of sugar, ¾ pint of milk or cream. Flour crust and bake until set. K. E. S.

Molasses Doughnuts—One cup of molasses, ½ cup of sugar, 1 egg, 1 cup of sour milk, 1 teaspoonful soda, pinch of salt, little nutmeg, 1 teaspoonful hot lard, enough flour to make a soft dough. Fry in hot lard.
MRS. HOWARD RICH.

PUDDINGS and DESSERTS

The proof of the pudding is the eating.

Dennison Pudding—One cup of butter, 1 cup of New Orleans molasses, 2 eggs, 1 cup seedless raisins, 1 cup currants, 3 cups of flour, 1 teaspoonful soda dissolved in hot water, 1 tablespoonful cloves, 1 tablespoonful cinnamon, 1 teaspoonful salt. Work butter and molasses together. Put in moulds and steam 3½ hours.

Sauce for Pudding—One cup of butter, 2 cups of sugar, 1 tablespoonful cornstarch, ½ grated nutmeg, 2 eggs, 1 cup of sherry and ½ cup of whisky. Pour over whole of this 1 pint of boiling water.   MRS. WILSON ROTHERMEL.

Ashburton Pudding—Four cups of flour, 1 cup of suet, chopped fine, 3 cups of raisins seeded, 1 cup of molasses, 1 cup of milk, 1 teaspoonful soda, dissolved in milk. Mix well and boil 3 hours in a large bag or mould.

Sauce for Pudding—One-fourth pound butter melted, ¾ pound of sugar, 2 eggs well beaten, 1 tumbler of sherry wine. Cook in double boiler until creamy.
                    MRS. WM. BRUSSTAR.

Apple or Peach Dumplings (Six Dumplings)—One pint of flour sifted with 1 heaping teaspoonful baking powder and a pinch of salt. Piece of butter size of an egg, rubbed into flour. Enough milk to make a soft dough. Roll into an oblong shaped piece about the thickness of pie crust. Cut into six long narrow strips. Lay on the fruit cut into small pieces or slices, and sprinkle with sugar. Roll each strip and stand on end in a pan, giving them plenty of room. Pour into the pan a syrup made of ½ cup of sugar, 1 teaspoonful of butter. Fill the cup with boiilng water. Bake the dumplings in this syrup from 20 minutes to ½ hour.
                    MIRIAM GEIGER YOUNG.

Brown Bread—Two cups of corn meal, 1½ cups of flour, 2 cups of milk, 1 cup of molasses, 1 teaspoonful soda, 1 teaspoonful salt and 1 tablespoon of lard (melted). Steam 3 hours and set in oven a few minutes to dry.

DIAMOND PONDS, 1899.

Corn Bread—One cup yellow corn meal, 1 cup of wheat flour, ½ cup granulated sugar, ½ teaspoon salt, 2 teaspoonfuls baking powder, 1 large cup of milk, 2 eggs, 1 tablespoonful butter. Sift flour meal, sugar, salt and powder, three times. Put in butter with hands, add milk, then eggs. Bake 25 minutes in moderate oven. If made exactly this way it never fails.

MRS. CHARLES REA, York.

Tea Cake—One cup of sugar, 1 tablespoon butter, 2 eggs, 1 cup of milk, 3 teaspoonfuls baking powder. Flavor with a little nutmeg. Bake in cake pans. Put little lumps of butter over the top, and sprinkle with sugar and cinnamon before baking.   MRS. E. G. STEACY.

Cinnamon Buns—Three tablespoonfuls butter, 3 tablespoonfuls sugar, 1 tablespoonful salt, 2-3 quart milk, 1 cake of Fleischmans Yeast, water or potato water, 3 pounds King Midas flour, 6 eggs (well beaten), 3 tablespoonfuls baking powder (heaping), 1 pound of butter, ½ ounce cinnamon, ¼ pound currants, 1 pound raisins, 5 pounds dark brown sugar. Scald the butter, sugar, salt and milk. Let it cool until it is luke-warm. Then add the yeast cake, and sufficient water or potato water to make an even quart. Pour into bread mixer and add flour, turn 5 minutes, set in warm place to raise until morning. In the morning, add the well beaten eggs, baking powder and sufficient flour to make a soft dough. Roll to a long length, and spread with butter, sprinkle with cinnamon, currants, raisins, and dark brown sugar. Roll and cut as you would cut jelly roll. Bake in a slow oven; turn out on a platter greased with butter. Dip up with a spoon the syrup that has run into the tins and pour over the buns. When cool, turn right side up and put the syrup which remains in the platter over the top of the buns. The above recipe makes 6 tins of 8 buns each.   PRISCILLA SELTZER,
President of Woman's Club.

SMALL CAKES

Drop Cakes—One pound granulated sugar, ½ pound butter, 4 eggs, 1¼ cups of thick milk, 1¼ pounds of flour, 1 teaspoonful baking powder dissolved in hot water, pour water off, add soda to thick milk, 1 pound small seedless raisins or currants. Cream sugar and butter, add eggs, then milk with soda, and flour and raisins. Drop on tins and bake a light brown.   SUSAN BEARD.

Peanut Wafers—One cup of soft white sugar, ½ cup of butter, ¾ cup of milk, 1 quart of peanuts crushed. Spread very thinly on sheets of iron, sprinkle thickly with the crushed nuts and bake in a hot oven.   MARGARET HODGES.

Boston Buns—One egg, 1 teaspoonful sugar, butter size of an egg, 1 cup of milk, 2 cups of flour, 2 teaspoonfuls baking powder. Drop on greased tins with spoon.
                                    MRS. WM. DECHANT.

Hermits—Three eggs, 1½ cups of sugar, 1 cup of butter, 1 cup of raisins ground, 2 tablespoonfuls of sour milk, 1 teaspoonful of soda, 1 teaspoonful of cinnamon, ½ nutmeg, flour enough to roll out and cut. Bake in quick oven.
                                    MRS. FRED ROWEN,
                                        Diamond Ponds.

Jumbles—Two cups of sugar, 1 cup of butter, ½ cup of sour milk 2 eggs, 1 teaspoonful baking powder, 4 cups of flour. Drop on tins and brush with egg, sugar and cinnamon.
                            MRS. WILSON ROTHERMEL.

Fruit Cookies—One-half cup of butter, ¾ cup of sugar, 2 eggs beaten separately, ½ teaspoonful cinnamon, 1 teaspoonful cloves, ½ teaspoonful soda in ¼ cup hot water, 1½ cups of flour, 1 cup of nut meats, ½ pound chopped dates, ½ pound seedless raisins, a little lemon juice. Drop on tins and bake quickly.   MRS. W. E. FISK.

Invalid's Tray

Remember the sick, and visit them.

CEREALS

Gruel—One cup liquid, 1 tablespoon flour or meal, 1-6 teaspoonful salt, 3 tablespoonfuls powdered crackers will be needed for 1 cup of liquid.

Gluten Mush—Three cups boiling water, 1 cup of cold water, 1 teaspoonful salt, 2-3 cup gluten flour. Add the cold water gradually to the flour, then pour through a strainer into the boiling salted water; cook 30 minutes, stirring frequently; strain.

Boiled Oats or Wheat—Three cups boiling water, 1 teaspoonful salt, 1 cup of meal. Boil 10 minutes stirring constantly and cook over boiling water at least 1½ hours longer, a better flavor is developed by longer cooking.

Irish Oatmeal—Four cups boiling water, 1 teaspoonful salt, 1 cup meal. Boil 10 minutes, stirring constantly, and then 8 hours over boiling water.

Corn Meal Mush—Four cups boiling water, 1 teaspoonful salt, 1 cup corn meal. Boil 10 minutes, stirring constantly, and 3 hours or longer over boiling water.

Steamed Rice—Two cups of boiling water, 1 teaspoonful salt, 1 cup of rice. Rice must be carefully picked over and washed thoroughly. Put rice water and salt into a bowl, place it in a steamer over rapidly boiling water. Cook until the rice is soft from ¾ to 1 hour.

Coffee Jelly—One-fourth package gelatine, ¼ cup cold water, 2½ cups coffee, ½ cup sugar. Soak the gelatine in the cold water, add the boiling coffee and sugar; strain.

Cherry Soup—For this most invigorating hot weather soup sweet or sour cherries may be used; preferably sour; 1 quart stoned cherries, 1 quart water, sugar to taste. Boil until cherries are transparent; thicken by adding 1 heaping tablespoonful of corn starch moistened with cold water. Boil until clear and serve piping hot to get best tonic effects. Not to be despised ice cold. This quantity will serve 8 persons.

MARTHA WEIS KASE.

Updated Version
Serves 4

Ingredients:
2½ cups water
1 cinnamon stick
1 teaspoon lemon juice
¼ cup sugar
¼ cup red wine
1 pound fresh (pitted) or frozen (thawed) cherries
½ plain yogurt

Directions:
Put water, cinnamon stick, lemon juice, sugar, and wine in a pot on the stove and bring to a boil. Add the cherries and reduce the heat. Cover, and let simmer for five minutes, then remove from heat. Once the liquid has cooled, slowly add it to a bowl containing the yogurt, mixing well. Put the soup in the refrigerator until chilled, about an hour. Before serving, mix the soup once more.

Club House Cook Book

(1904)

The *Club House Cook Book* was published by the Tuesday Club of Sacramento in 1904. Organized in 1896, the Tuesday Club was a member of the California Federation of Women's Clubs, the General Federation of Women's Clubs, and the Woman's Council of Sacramento. Founded by Mrs. Finley R. Dray, it met in the original Elk's Building.

Favorite Recipes

COLLECTED BY

The Tuesday Club House Ass'n

OF SACRAMENTO, CALIFORNIA

Within the covers of this book will be found recipes for all kinds of "tasty dishes." Each one offered has been tested by competent housewives......It is put forth with the certain belief that a fair trial will prove it to have a genuine and permanent place among books of its kind . . . .

SOUPS

The first and most important point in making good soup is to have the best of materials. Soft cold water is necessary, and it should not boil but simmer, and should always be made in a porcelain-lined or granite soup-kettle.

SOUP STOCK.

1 shin of beef,
5 qts. cold water,
1 onion,
1 carrot,
1 turnip,
2 bay leaves,
1 sprig parsley,
12 cloves,
1 stock celery,
1 tablespoon salt.

Cut the meat from the bones, and place the bones in the bottom of the kettle, lay the meat on top of them, add water and stand on the back part of the range for one hour. Then place over a good fire. Soon the scum will form on top. Skim, cover kettle closely and let it simmer (not boil) four hours. Then add vegetables and simmer one hour longer. Strain, add salt and put at once in a cool place. When cold take all the grease from the surface and it is ready for use.   *Mrs. S. T. Rorer.*

EGG BARLEY SOUP.

soup bone,
bunch of soup
* vegetables,*
2 green peppers,
3 eggs,
salt and pepper,
½ doz. cloves.

Take a large soup bone with all kinds of vegetables (the onion stuck with cloves), and allow to simmer five hours and strain; add salt and pepper. In soup-tureen beat eggs very light and add the boiling stock. Stir constantly.   *Mrs. J. M. Merritt.*

POTATO SALAD.

(*Cooked Mayonnaise.*)

3 tbsp. vinegar,
2 eggs,
butter,
1 level tsp. salt,
½ tsp. dry mustard,
⅛ tsp. cayenne,
2 lemons (juice),
1 onion (grated),
parsley.

Potatoes should be boiled on the morning of the day salad is to be used, but not sliced until cold.

DRESSING.—Heat vinegar to boiling in agate cup. Beat yolks of eggs and pour hot vinegar over them and stir smooth; return to the agate cup, place on fire, stirring constantly until thick (quite stiff). Upon removing from the fire, add lump of butter and stir. Into a dry cup put salt, mustard and cayenne. Stir all together dry, and squeeze into this the juice of lemons and mix with onion. Pour this over the egg and vinegar, stir until smooth; then add cream and stir until dressing is consistency of thick root. Add the well-beaten whites of eggs at the last, and when dressing has been poured over sliced potatoes and salad lightly tossed with a fork, sprinkle minced parsley over all. Celery root, chopped very fine, is quite a pleasant addition. Enough for six persons.

Mrs. G. W. Lorenz.

FRENCH DRESSING.

2 tbsp. oil,
1 tbsp. vinegar,
1 saltspoon salt.

Mix well together. You can use lemon juice instead of vinegar.

OYSTERS FRIED IN OIL.

24 *oysters,*
2 *eggs,*
2 *tbsp. hot water.*

Drain oysters and dry with cheese cloth. Dust with salt and cayenne. Beat eggs and add hot water. Dip oysters first in bread crumbs, then quickly in egg and back in the crumbs. Lift the oysters singly with the fingers and place singly on a board. Have oil or lard smoking hot. Place oysters in wire basket (five or six only at a time), sink basket in hot fat and cook until a golden brown. Lift carefully and place on brown paper in baking-pan, and fry the remaining quantity. Garnish with lemon and parsley and serve very hot.

Mrs. Rorer.

FISH TIMBALL.

2 *lbs. sea-bass or*
sturgeon,
¼ *loaf bread,*
¼ *lb. butter,*
4 *eggs,*
cayenne salt and a
little lime juice,
½ *pt. sweet cream.*

Boil fish, shred (save water in which it was boiled) and remove bones. Soak bread in water and squeeze dry. Mix fish with bread, butter, eggs, cayenne, salt and lime juice, and last the cream. Beat very light for half an hour. Butter mold and boil hard one hour. Serve very hot with sauce made with water fish was boiled in, and mushrooms.

Mrs. Emil Steinman.

TARTER SAUCE FOR SALMON.

2 *egg yolks,*
1 *tbsp. French*
vinegar,
parsley,
1 *gill olive oil,*
1 *tbsp. French*
mustard,
salt,
a few gherkins, or
capers.

Beat eggs and salt and add oil drop by drop; then add chopped parsley, mustard, vinegar and capers.

Mrs. L. McGavigan.

ENTREES

"The turnpike road to people's hearts, I find,
Lies through their mouths, or I mistake mankind."

100 *oysters,*
2 *limes (juice),*
1 *tbsp. Worcester-*
  shire sauce,
6 *tbsp. tomato*
  catsup,
1 *tbsp. vinegar,*
2 *tsp. pepper,*
salt, dash tobasco.

OYSTER COCKTAILS.

(*For Six Persons.*)

Select small California oysters, mix all together and serve.

Mrs. J. D. Powell.

2 *oz. butter,*
3 *small onions,*
2 *green peppers,*
salt, red pepper,
1 *tomato,*
1 *tbsp. flour,*
½ *c. cream.*

CRAB CREOLE (*For Six*).

Chop onions and peppers (without seeds) very fine and put in stew-pan with butter, salt and red pepper. Stew slowly ten minutes and add tomato (peeled). Stew this until dissolved. Add flour mixed with cream and make it thick as drawn butter. Put in finely picked crab. Serve on toast.

Mrs. F. R. Dray.

1 *tsp. English*
  mustard,
2 *tsp. Parisian*
  sauce,
⅓ *tsp. red pepper,*
1 *tsp. salt.*

BRAINS DEVILED.

Clean brains until white by picking off the skins in cold water. Mix mustard, Parisian sauce, red pepper and salt together. Into this mixture roll brains; then into bread crumbs and fry, until brown on both sides, in a frying-pan. Over this pour enough water to make gravy, and boil about ten minutes. Thicken gravy to taste and serve hot.

Mrs. William Beckman.

PORK CHOPS.

If chops are very fat, remove all but a quarter inch of fat; season with salt and pepper. Fry chops and portion of removed fat brown. Afterward pour boiling water over chops, adding half a teaspoonful of mustard. Simmer for three-quarters of an hour. Make paste of tablespoonful of flour and thin with a cup of milk. Pour paste over chops, boiling five minutes, adding a small wine-glass of sherry just before removing. *Mrs. J. J. Keegan.*

SPANISH.

4 tomatoes,
1 onion,
3 peppers,
1 clove garlic,
salt, butter, pepper,
Worcester sauce.

Chop up fine and cook well.
Mrs. J. D. Powell.

BAKED TONGUE.

1 beef tongue,
1 egg,
cracker crumbs.

Boil tongue one hour (not hard) and add salt. Boil another hour. Take up and skin, removing all rough parts. Beat egg and roll tongue in egg and cracker crumbs. Lay in pan and season well with salt and pepper. Add one pint of water in which it has been boiled, and bake. Baste well while baking, and serve with a good gravy or cream sauce. *Mrs. L. McGavigan.*

SWEETBREADS.

½ doz. sweetbreads,
1 egg,
1 c. cream,

Scald sweetbreads in salt water; take out the stringy parts. Leave a few

a little flour,
truffles,
parsley,
salt, pepper.

moments in cold water, then dry and roll in egg and bread crumbs. Fry brown in butter. To gravy add a little flour, a few truffles, parsley, salt, pepper and cream. Pour over sweetbreads and serve hot. *Mrs. L. McG——.*

CHRISTMAS DISH.

Cover the bottom of a pudding dish with fine bread crumbs, lay on bits of butter, then a layer of cold boiled eggs, sliced; then a layer of cold turkey or chicken, cut fine. Add pepper and salt. Repeat until the dish is full. Cover with bread crumbs and moisten cream or milk and bake.

Mrs. E. S——.

KIDNEY SAUTE WITH WINE.

kidneys,
1 onion,
salt,
pepper,
parsley,
½ lemon.

Cut kidneys into slices and cook ten minutes in a frying-pan in drippings (or oil). Take up and lay on a hot-water dish, covering closely. Add to the drippings in the pan a little gravy (beef will do) or a little soup. Season with chopped onion, parsley, salt and pepper, and thicken with browned flour. Boil up; add a glass of good wine and juice of lemon. Pour over the kidneys and set in boiling water five minutes. If kidneys are cooked too long they toughen. *Mrs. L. McG——.*

CRUMPETS.

1 qt. light sponge,
5 eggs.

Take sponge from your bread, break eggs in one at a time, beat light and add milk-warm water until a batter as thin as for buckwheat cakes is formed.

Mrs. E. P. Howe.

WAFFLES.

1 qt. flour,
1 c. cream,
2 tsp. bak'g powder,
2 eggs,
salt,
milk.

Sift baking powder with flour; add well-beaten eggs, cream, salt and enough milk to make the right consistency to spread in the waffle-iron well.

Mrs. F. A. Edinger.

CREAM BISCUITS.

1 qt. flour,
1½ tsp. baking
   powder,
¾ c. pastry cream,
salt,
milk.

Sift flour, baking powder and salt together; add cream and milk enough to make a soft dough. Knead lightly with the tips of fingers one minute. Cut with very small cutter and bake in quick oven.   *Mrs. F. A. Edinger.*

TEA BISCUITS.

1 qt. flour,
1 tsp. bak'g powder,
2 tbsp. butter,
1 tbsp. lard,
pinch of salt,
milk.

Mix all together quickly and bake in a quick oven.   *Mrs. E. S.*

CHEESED CRACKERS.

butter,
crackers,
cheese,
salt,
pepper.

Butter crackers and place in large dripping-pan; sprinkle heavily with grated cheese; salt and red pepper to taste. Put in oven until hot.

Mrs. F. A. E.

PUDDINGS AND DESSERTS

"The proof of the pudding is the eating."

CARROT PUDDING.

1 c. grated carrots,
1 c. grated potatoes,
1 c. brown sugar,
1 c. raisins,
1 c. currants,
1 c. suet,
2 eggs,
1½ c. flour,
a pinch of soda.

Chop suet fine and mix all the ingredients together and steam or boil two and one-half hours.

Mrs. E. E. Earle.

HONEY COMB PUDDING.

½ c. flour,
½ c. milk,
1 tbsp. butter,
4 eggs,
½ c. sugar,
1 c. molasses,
1 tsp. soda

Beat yolks very light and mix with sugar, salt and molasses. Then mix with milk, melted butter and well beaten whites of eggs. Last, the soda. Bake in a shallow pan forty minutes.

1 large c. sugar,
1 egg,
1 c. butter,
1 lemon,
1 tsp. nutmeg
6 tbsp. boiling water

SAUCE.—Cream butter and sugar. Beat egg very light and add to cream. and beat, add nutmeg, water and last the juice and half grated rind of a lemon. Put on the stove a few minutes and stir constantly.

Mrs. F. A. Johnson.

CHOCOLATE PUDDING.

1 c. sugar,
½ c. butter,
1 c. flour,
4 eggs,
1 tsp. bak'g powder,
1 c. chocolate,
½ c. sherry wine,
1 tsp. cinnamon,
¼ tsp. nutmeg,
1 tsp. vanilla.

Beat the eggs together and mix with the chocolate; add the other ingredients and steam. Serve with whipped cream.

Mrs. C. M. Beckwith.

PLUM PUDDING.

½ lb. bread crumbs
½ lb. suet, chopped
    fine,
½ lb. currants,
½ lb. chop'd apples
    (more if desired),
½ lb. raisins (more
    if desired),
1 c. sugar,
1 grated nutmeg,
2 oz. candied orange
    peel,
1 tsp. salt,
1 tsp. cloves,
2 tsp. cinnamon,
4 eggs, well beaten,
1 c. milk,
1 tsp. soda.

In a large bowl put the eggs, sugar, spices and salt in one cupful of milk. Stir in the other ingredients one after the other, having first floured the fruit. Next, add the soda dissolved in a little hot water, then enough flour to make all hold together. Boil four or five hours.   *Mrs. S. B. Slight.*

LEMON CREAM.

8 eggs,
8 tbsp. sugar,
2 lemons,
1 c. water,
1 glass wine.

Beat yolk of eggs very light, add sugar, water, wine, juice of lemons and rind of one. Allow this to simmer (not boil) till it thickens. Remove from fire and add the white of eggs that have been beaten stiff, and one cup of sugar. Serve cold in glasses.

Mrs. C. M. Beckwith.

BROWN BETTY OR BAKED APPLE JUDY.

bread crumbs,
apples, sliced,
butter,
sugar,
spices.

Take well-buttered baking pan and put in a layer of bread crumbs, dotting them over with small lumps of butter, then a layer of apples; sweeten and spice to taste. Repeat until the dish is full, having bread crumbs on top. If the apples are not very juicy, add a little boiling water to the whole.

Mrs. James T. Martin.

TOMATO RELISH (*Splendid*).

2 c. chopped onions,
2 c. chopped celery,
2 c. brown sugar,
1 c. white mustard
    seed,
2 tsp. cinnamon,
2 tsp. cloves,
4 red peppers,
½ tsp. pepper,
3 pts. vinegar,
2 c. salt.

Eight quarts ripe tomatoes, chopped fine; cover with salt and drain in a bag over night. Next morning add all the other ingredients, and pack in jars with horse-radish on top.

Mrs. E. L. Hawk.

PICKLED ONIONS.

Clean the small button onions thoroughly, cover with hot brine, let stand over night, then drain and cover with hot vinegar, spiced to taste.

Mrs. Rorer.

CHOW–CHOW (*Excellent*).

4 pecks green toma-
    toes,
1 small head cab-
    bage,
½ doz. cucumbers,
½ doz. large onions,
½ doz. green pep-
    pers,
1 c. salt.
2 qts. vinegar,
2 c. sugar,
1 tbsp. cloves,
1 tbsp. allspice,
1 tbsp. cinnamon,
1 tbsp. black pepper,
1 tbsp. nutmeg,
1 tbsp. mustard,
2 tbsp yellow mus-
    tard seed.

Chop tomatoes, cabbage, cucumbers, onions and peppers fine and mix with salt, place in stone jar and stand over night. Next morning put in a bag and drain dry; put back in the jar and cover with vinegar, and let stand over night and drain again. Now take vinegar and add sugar, cloves, alspice, cinnamon, pepper, nutmeg, mustard and mustard seed. Mix together thoroughly; if not moist enough, add a little more sweetened vinegar; put in glass jar; will keep indefinately.

Mrs William Irving, Colfax.

Favorite Recipes

(1923)

Favorite Recipes was published in 1923 by the Young Woman's Auxiliary of the Congregational Church of LaGrange, Illinois (now the First Congreational Church). The church was gathered March 18, 1881, when 17 charter members covenanted to form a congregation. Part of the present building was built in 1892 and is located at the corner of LaGrange Road and Cossitt Avenue.

Favorite Recipes

Compiled by

Young Woman's Auxiliary
of the
Congregational Church

La Grange, Illinois

December, Nineteen Twenty-three

SOUPS

Though fortunes frown and skies are drear,
And friends are changing year by year,
One thing is always sure to please,
Just give him soups such as these.

CORN CHOWDER

2 thin slices of salt pork   1 cup of canned corn
4 small potatoes   Salt and pepper
1 cup of hot water   1 teaspoon of butter
¾ of a quart of milk

Fry out the pork, add potatoes diced, cook in cup of hot water until potatoes are done. Add corn, butter and seasoning, lastly the milk and heat well but not boiling.—Mrs. H. H. Holton.

CREAM VEGETABLE SOUPS

4 tablespoons of cooked peas, asparagus or potatoes
2 cups of water, the vegetables were cooked in

In case canned vegetables are used, use all the water in the can, and rice the vegetables into it, adding enough water to make 2 cups in all.

2 cups milk   1 tablespoon flour
1 tablespoon butter   1 teaspoon salt
Paprika

Let all the ingregients come to a boil and thicken with the flour and a little cold water.—Margaret T. Vial.

VEGETABLE BROTH

¾ lb. round steak   2 tomatoes
1 stalk celery   2 carrots
2 onions

Cut steak in small cubes, cover with two quarts of cold water, put over very slow flame and when it boils add vegetables. Cook clowly until they are soft. Time required is about three hours. Add salt and pepper when nearly done. —Margaret E. Thompson.

OYSTER SOUP

1 quart milk   1 quart oysters
Heat milk

Cook oysters in 1 pint of water until they begin to curl, add seasoning, butter, salt and pepper. Then add hot milk and serve at once. Soup made this way will not curdle.— Mrs. Gaylord.

CREAM OF TOMATO SOUP

1 can of tomatoes (strained). Cook to boiling point, then add pinch (½ teaspoon soda) before pouring tomatoes into milk that has come to a boiling point. Make thickening of butter and flour and add to soup. Season to taste. Do not make it too thick, just enough to give it body.—Mrs. J. E. Edmonds.

CREAM OF CELERY SOUP

Cut off tops and outside pieces of six stalks or more of celery; chop or cut it finely with two carrots and one small onion. Add 1 pint can of tomatoes or 3 fresh ones, 2 cloves, a small piece of bay leaf, a little mace, salt and pepper and 1 pint of water. Boil slowly for 1 hour, drain through colander or sieve. For cream, run together and brown slightly 1 tablespoon each of butter and flour. Add 1 pint of milk and cook slowly for a few minutes, then add to first mixture and serve immediately—Mrs. J. E. Bratt.

CARROT SOUP

2 cups of carrots cut in small pieces	1 tablespoon of butter
3 cups of water	1 tablespoon of flour
½ small green pepper, chopped fine	Salt and pepper
3 cups of milk or part cream	1 slice of onion

Boil carrots until tender, press through sieve using water that remains. Scald onion in milk and remove. Cream butter and flour, add to milk. Combine with carrot liquid. Allow to boil a second. Add finely chopped green pepper, boil a few seconds longer.—Mrs. Albert Heppes.

CREAM OF BEET SOUP

2 tablespoons butter with 3 tablespoons flour and add to 3 pints of milk. 1½ cups beets boiled and mashed. Boil together and add to beets, adding salt and pepper to taste.

HALIBUT BAKED IN CUSTARD (Four Portions)

1 lb. halibut	1 small onion
2 tablespoons flour	1 teaspoon salt
1 cup milk	¼ teaspoon paprika
2 eggs	⅛ teaspoon pepper
1 tablespoon minced parsley	2 tablespoons grated cheese
	1 tablespoon butter

Purchase 1 slice halibut weighing about 1 lb. Cut the fish into 6 filets, removing the bones. Lay the filets into a buttered, shallow baking dish and sprinkle with ½ teaspoon salt, the parsley, paprika and the onion grated. In a bowl, beat the eggs slightly and add the flour, milk, remaining salt, and pepper. Beat together to blend and pour over the fish. Bake at 350° F. for ½ hour or until set.—Etta S. Tyler.

FISH SOUFFLE

Put 1 cup of stale bread crumbs and ½ cup of milk over the fire, stir constantly until boiling hot, take from fire and add yolks of 2 eggs, ¼ teaspoon salt, same amount of pepper, stir into this 1 cup of shredded codfish, when well mixed, stir in carefully whites of 2 eggs beaten to a stiff froth, put quickly into baking dish and bake in a quick oven 5 minutes or until golden brown. Serve at once.—Mrs. John Windsor.

CREAMED SHRIMP

Heat 1 can (small) of shrimps in a tablespoon of butter, stirring until warmed through but not browned; add ¼ tablespoon of onion extract or onion juice. 1 gill of milk and 6 beaten eggs stirred in and cooked until the consistency of rich cream. Serve at once on squares of toast or toasted crackers. Nice for chafing dish and onion may be omitted if desired.—Mrs. John Windsor.

SHRIMP WIGGLE

1 can shrimp	1 can French peas
	1 doz. olives chopped fine

Melt 1 tablespoon butter in dish. Add 2 tablespoons flour and 2 cups milk. Cook, season to taste, then add shrimp, peas and olives. Serve at once on toast.—Mrs. James A. Walker.

MOCK LOBSTER NEWBERG

1 cup of tomatoes stewed with ½ teaspoon sugar; add 1 scant cup dried beef shredded and 1 heaping cup grated cheese. When the cheese is melted add 1 egg slightly beaten and cook 1 minute. Red pepper should be added to taste.—May B. Judd.

FRICASSIED OYSTERS

1 qt. oysters, drain as dry as possible, butter size of an egg, put in spider and get quite brown, add oysters and as soon as they cook a minute, add as much more butter, which has been well mixed with a tablespoon of flour. Cook a minute and add 1 egg beaten with 2 tablespoon of cream. Let the whole cook a bit and pour over toasted bread.—Mrs. George M. Vial.

HOLLENDEN HALIBUT

Arrange 6 thin slices of fat salt pork in a dripping pan. Cover with 1 small onion thinly sliced and add a bit of bay leaf. Wipe a 2-lb. slice of halibut and place on the onion and pork. Cream 3 tablespoons butter and 3 of flour and spread on the fish. Cover with ¾ cup of buttered cracker crumbs and arrange thin strips of fat salt pork over the crumbs. Cover and bake 50 minutes in moderate oven removing the cover the last 15 minutes to brown the crumbs. Remove to hot serving dish and garnish with thin slices of lemon and sprinkle with paprika.—Mrs. W. R. Eastman.

CREAMED SHRIMP ON TOAST

1 can wet shrimp or	1 pint milk
1 pint fresh shrimp	Salt
1 tablespoon butter	Pepper
2 tablespoons flour	Paprika

Pimento to taste

Cut shrimp in small pieces, melt butter, add flour and milk. Let cook until it thickens, add shrimp and the salt, pepper, paprika and pimento to taste and serve very hot on toast.—Mrs. F. M. Bartlett.

MEATS

Did you say mutton or sausage or ham
Or nice green peas with mint sauce and lamb?
Tastes are varied, but let me make
This observation; you'll not mistake
In chosing a sirloin, a very good one
Like all good things—not overdone.

FRICASSEE CHICKEN

Cut chicken in pieces and dredge with flour. Season with salt and celery salt. Brown in spider with large lump of butter or bacon fat. When brown on both sides cover with boiling water and boil until done. Thicken the gravy and serve.—Mrs. Wm. H. Moore.

ESCALLOPED VEAL

Cook the veal, also the bones and trimmings, in a small amount of water. When tender, drain in colander, put the stock back on the fire, season it, and thicken to proper gravy consistency with flour and butter rubbed together. (Seasoning for veal should always include a little lemon juice.) Then cut the veal into small pieces, arrange a layer in a buttered baking dish, cover with bread crumbs, and moisten well with gravy. Arrange the second layer likewise, finishing with crumbs moistened with melted butter. Bake brown. Oysters may be substituted for the crumb layers, and makes a delicious dish. Spiced gooseberries are nice served with veal.—Berenice Kissick.

ITALIAN STYLE VEAL CHOPS

3 loin or rib veal chops	2 carrots
1 green pepper	2 tablespoons shortening
1 spanish onion	Salt and pepper to taste

3 large tomatoes or ½ can tomatoes

Brown veal chops in shortening, then add vegetables, either sliced thin or chopped and allow to simmer for 1 hour. The sauce is delicious either thickened with flour or with cream added.—Mrs. H. D. Kelso.

SPANISH CHICKEN

Cut up a young chicken as for frying. Put in a kettle that can be closely covered and add:

1 can mushrooms (without the juice) or fresh mushrooms	
1 can peas with juice	1 sweet pepper cut fine
1 can tomatoes	A little red pepper

Salt, pepper and plenty of butter

Bake 1½ hours.—Althea L. Godso.

SWEDISH MEAT CAKES

1 lb. round steak, ground   1 small onion, grated
2 egg yolks or 1 egg   1 teaspoon lemon juice or
¾ cup soft bread crumbs   Worcester sauce
½ cup milk or stock   Salt and pepper

Mix lightly. Make into cakes, roll in flour and brown in fat in skillet. Add 1½ cups of tomato sauce or stock. Put in covered casserole and bake 45 minutes. Serve with a border of rice.—Mrs. Robt. Frey.

CROQUETTES

Two small cups veal or chicken (chopped)
12 large oysters, chopped
1 cup bread crumbs cooked in 1½ cups milk
1 egg
Pepper and salt to taste

Mold in cone shape, dip in egg, then cracker meal, and fry in hot lard.—Mrs. Fred S. Lodge.

PORK AND NOODLES

1 lb. lean pork shoulder, cut in small pieces and fried
2 medium sized onions, fried
1 package Broad (real egg noodles) cooked

Mix all together and add 1 can of Campbell's tomato soup. If not moist enough add a little hot water. Bake 1 hour in a casserole.—Mrs. A. M. Hawkins.

VEGETABLE LOAF

1 lb. of beef, ground   1 egg
¼ lb. of pork, ground   ½ cup chopped celery
1 cup bread crumbs   ½ cup chopped tomatoes
             Salt to taste

A little catsup if desired. Bake in casserole.—Florelle G. Hawley.

VEAL LOAF (Very Good)

3½ lbs. of raw veal   Butter, size of an egg
½ lb. of salt pork, chopped fine 3 eggs
3 tablespoons of cream or milk 1 teaspoon of black pepper
3½ tablespoons of cracker meal 1 large tablespoon of salt
         1 large tablespoon of sage

Mix well together, form into loaf. Put small slices of onion over top and bake 2½ hours.—Margaret A. Randall.

MEAT LOAF

½ lb. of beef, ground   ½ teaspoon grated nutmeg
½ lb. of pork, ground   1 teaspoon salt
½ cup of cracker crumbs 1 teaspoon baking powder,
½ cup canned tomatoes   (mix with cracker crumbs)
½ cup of cream or milk 1 well beaten egg
½ can mushrooms   1 large onion
1 pimento or green pepper ½ teaspoon pepper
        1 teaspoon of sugar

Bake in moderate oven 30-40 minutes. Oil the pan. Cover at first, uncover to brown. Serves 6.—Mrs. E. E. Crook.

MEAT LOAF

1½ lbs. chopped beef   ½ cup tomato soup
½ lb. chopped pork   1 tablespoon minced onion
1½ teaspoons salt   ½ cup bread or cracker crumbs
½ teaspoon pepper   1 egg

Mix well and bake 1 hour in greased loaf pan.—Mrs. George M. Stevens.

MEAT LOAF (3 lbs.)

1 lb. veal, ground   2 eggs
1 lb. ham, ground   1½ cups bread crumbs
1 lb. beef, ground   2 cups milk

Mix together, add 1 teaspoon baking powder and season with sage, black pepper, parsley, onion and salt. Bake in moderate oven 1 to 1½ hours.—Mrs. Byron Greenlee.

VEGETABLES

There is in every cook's opinion no savory dish without an onion. But lest your kissing should be spoiled the onion must be thoroughly boiled.

BOSTON BAKED BEANS

1 pint beans	1/8 teaspoon mustard
1/2 lb. fat salt pork	1/8 teaspoon soda
1/2 teaspoon salt	2 tablespoons molasses

Soak beans over night in water to more than cover. In morning drain. Put all in baking dish with pork in center, cover well with cold water and bake at least eight hours. As they dry out hot water should be added, a little at a time, until last hour, when they should be allowed to brown.

A small oven placed on top of single gas burner is very good in which to bake beans.—Georgia H. Duclos.

BOSTON BAKED BEANS

1 1/2 pounds beans   1 tablespoon dark brown sugar

1 tablespoon molasses

or

2 tablespoons dark brown sugar   1/2 teaspoon baking soda

1/2 teaspoon salt   3/4 pound salt pork

Soak beans over night, drain, cover with fresh water and 1/2 teaspoon of soda. Bring to a boil and let boil one hour on a very slow fire. Drain, add sugar, molasses, salt and salt pork. Bury the pork until just the rind can be seen. Cover with boiling water and bake 8 hours on a very slow fire, adding enough water from time to time to keep it moist but not floating.—Mrs F M Bartlett

BEETS WITH SAUCE

Mix 1/2 cup sugar and 1/2 tablespoon corn starch, add 1/2 cup vinegar, boil 5 minutes, add 2 tablespoons butter To this sauce add 1 pint cooked beets, cut in small cubes, (measure after cutting). Let it stand 1/2 hour, reheat just before serving.—Mrs. George B. Horr.

PARSNIP CROQUETTES

Boil parsnips in salted water, then mash them. When cool add 1 tablespoon of butter, pinch of pepper and salt and 1 beaten egg. Make into croquettes, rolled in dried bread crumbs, dip in beaten egg, then in crumbs again. Fry in wire basked in deep fat to a delicate golden yellow.—Mrs. James Kelso.

CORN FRITTERS

1 egg	1 teaspoon baking powder
½ can corn	2 cups flour
1 cup milk	½ teaspoon salt

Mix in order given and drop from spoon into hot grease. —Mrs. K. C. Holman.

CORN, SOUTHERN FASHION

1 cup sweet milk	2 tablespoons butter, melted
1 can corn	2 eggs, well beaten

Salt and pepper to taste. Mix well and bake 30 minutes in greased pan.—Mrs. John W. Matthews.

BAKED CAULIFLOUR WITH CHEESE

Boil cauliflower unbroken until tender; drain and place in baking dish; blend 1 tablespoon of flour with 1 cup of milk and 1 tablespoon of butter and pour over cauliflower. Cover with bread crumbs seasoned with salt and pepper and grated cheese. Bake.—Bonnie S. Craig.

SCALLOPED BRUSSELS SPROUTS

Cook brussel sprouts in boiling salted water until tender. Drain and place in baking dish. Cover with cream sauce, sprinkle the top with bread crumbs and grated cheese. Bake in moderate oven until brown.—Jane Toates.

Breakfast Dishes

"Dinner may be pleasant;
So may social tea;
But yet, me thinks the breakfast
Is good enough for me."

FRENCH TOAST

Beat 2 eggs thoroughly, add ½ teaspoon salt, 1 table-spoon of sugar and ⅔ cup of milk. Mix well and pour into shallow dish or pan. Cut stale bread in thin slices, put one slice at a time in egg mixture, let soak about ½ minute, then brown on both sides in hot griddle. Serve hot with maple syrup, jam or honey.—Mrs. H. D. Kelso.

POPOVERS

Sift together 1 cup of flour and ¼ teaspoon of salt, add gradually ⅞ cups of milk, stirring constantly until a smooth batter is formed. Add 2 eggs beaten until thick and lemon tinted and ½ teaspoon of olive oil or melted butter. Beat with an egg-beater at least 2 minutes. Turn into buttered custard cups or iron gem cups and bake 35 minutes in hot oven.

The thick and heavier cups are much better for this purpose. The strongest heat must come evenly from the bottom of the oven and cups if you wish the mixture to puff well and popover. Serve hot.—Mrs. Durland.

FRENCH TOAST

2 eggs   ½ teaspoon salt
                      1 cup milk

Mix above ingredients well together. Dip a slice of bread into some of the mixture, which has been poured into a soup plate, continue adding mixture and dipping slices until a dozen have been used. Let stand; spread on a platter for half an hour, then toast on both sides. Serve very hot with powdered sugar.—Mildred N. Gibson.

RICE PANCAKES

1½ cups boiled rice   2 tablspoons sugar
2½ cups flour   Pinch of salt
2½ teaspoons baking powder   2 eggs

Small lump of melted butter, milk to make a thin batter. Serve hot with maple syrup.—Myrtle Powers.

LUNCHEON DISHES

Study simplicity in the number of dishes, and variety in the character of the meals.

CRAB TOAST

2 tablespoons butter	½ teaspoon pepper
1 tablespoon flour	1 pint crab meat
½ teaspoon mustard	1 teaspoon lemon juice
½ teaspoon salt	1 hard-boiled egg
	¾ cup of milk

Make white sauce of butter, flour, milk and seasonings in double boiler. Add lemon juice, diced eggs and crab meat. Mix well and serve on toast.—Mrs. O. F. Schultz.

TIMBALE OF SALMON

1 lb. can salmon	4 tablespoons cream
4 eggs	Salt and pepper to taste

Remove salmon from can, mash fine, adding cream, salt and pepper, and yolks of eggs well beaten. Beat the whites of the eggs to a stiff froth and stir them in. Fill greased cups ⅔ full and stand them in a pan of hot water. Bake 15 minutes in a quick oven. Serve with tomato sauce.—Margaret T. Vial.

CHOP SUEY

2 large stalks celery	1 can mushrooms
2 large onions	1 tablespoon molasses
1 lb. veal, cut fine	1 tablespoon flour
½ lb. pork, cut fine	1 cup water
	2 tablespoons Suey sauce

Cook meat 3 minutes in 3 tablespoons boiling fat, add celery and onions, sprinkle with flour, cook 10 minutes, add mushrooms, molasses, water and Suey sauce.—Mrs. R. P. Moore.

CREAMED CELERY ON TOAST

1 cup celery cooked in small pieces
2 hard-boiled eggs cut in slices

Cream sauce made of 2 cups milk, 1 tablespoon butter, 1 rounded tablespoon flour.—Mrs. Otto Heppes.

MACARONI AND CHEESE

1 box macaroni broken and boiled in salt water for 20 minutes and drained. Place in buttered pan a layer of macaroni, grated cheese, bits of butter, salt and pepper, and other layer of macaroni, etc., until pan is full. Beat one egg together with ¼ spoon mustard and fill cup with milk. Pour over macaroni and bake golden brown, about 25 minutes.—Mrs. F. H. Kasson.

BAKED MACARONI, BACON AND CORN

2 cups macaroni or spaghetti   ¼ teaspoon pepper
1 cup canned corn   ¼ teaspoon paprika
1 teaspoon salt   1½ cups white sauce
                    3 slices bacon

Cook macaroni until tender, drain and pour cold water through. Make white sauce by adding 1 level tablespoon flour to 1 tablespoon melted butter. Add to this 1½ cups milk and cook until thickened. Then add to this sauce the seasoning, corn and cooked macaroni. Put in a buttered baking dish and lay the slices of bacon cut in squares over the top. Bake in a hot oven fifteen or twenty minutes.—Georgia H. Duclos.

MACARONI SOUFFLE

Cream gravy with cheese   2 egg yolks
1½ tablespoons butter   1 pint milk
1½ tablespoons flour   1 cup grated cheese

Add to the cheese gravy after it is cooked, one large cupful of cooked macaroni, take off stove and fold in whites of two eggs. Serve hot. —Mrs. Wm. J. Herzog.

MACARONI SOUFFLE

1 cup macaroni cooked till done   1 cup cheese grated
1 cup bread crumbs   Little parsley and pimento
1 cup cream or milk   3 eggs beaten

Mix all together and bake in casserole 1 hour. Put casserole in dish of hot water.—Mrs. O. W. Bartlett.

CORN CAKE WITH BACON

Line shallow pan with tiny pieces of bacon. Pour over the following batter:

1 cup flour	2 teaspoons baking powder
1 cup corn meal	1 egg
½ cup sugar	1 cup milk
1 teaspoon salt	1 tablespoon melted lard

Bake about 25 minutes in hot oven.—Mrs. K. R. Elwell.

OLD SOUTHERN CORN BREAD

2 cups corn meal	1 egg (may be omitted)
1½ cups thick sour milk	1 teaspoon salt
3 teaspoons melted drippings	

Beat egg, add sour milk, sift in meal, add soda dissolved in a little hot water, salt and drippings. Beat well and pour into well greased pan. Bake in moderate oven.—Mrs. H. J. Jacobi.

OAT MEAL BREAD

2 cups quaker oats	1 cake yeast
1 qt. boiling water	⅔ cup molasses
1 tablespoon lard	1 teaspoon salt
2 quarts flour	

Pour boiling water on oats, add lard and salt, cool sufficiently to add yeast, add molasses and flour, let it rise, stir down, rise again, make into loaves, rise and bake 1 hour.—Mrs. Harry J. Ilett.

CORN BREAD

1½ cups milk	⅛ cup flour
2 tablespoons shortening	4 teaspoons baking powder
1¾ cups corn meal	1 tablespoon sugar
1 teaspoon salt	

—Mrs. M. W. Heath.

Desserts and Ices

The Proof of the Pudding is in the Eating
Of all known sauces, Hunger's the best
Doubtless this ancient saw is true
But give us Hunger and sauces too.

ENGLISH PLUM PUDDING

1 lb. finely chopped suet
1 lb. flour
1 lb. seeded raisins
1 lb. currants
1 lb. loaf bakers' bread
1¼ lb. sugar
2 heaping teaspoons baking powder
1 teaspoon salt
6 eggs

½ teaspoon cinnamon
½ teaspoon all spice
½ teaspoon nutmeg
¼ teaspoon ginger
1¼ teaspoons cloves
Juice ½ lemon and ½ orange
Candied orange
Candied lemon
Candied citron

Soak the bread, drain as dry as possible, add well beaten eggs, sugar and flour. Beat well, then add fruit and spices. This may be boiled or steamed. If to be steamed, put into 2 buttered milk crocks and steam over boiling water 6 hours. If boiled, take a square piece of cotton cloth, dip it in scalding hot water, flour it well and lay it over a pan. Place the pudding in the cloth and tie it closely. Put it into a pot of boiling water for 5 hours. Have boiling water ready to fill the pot as it boils away, so as not to allow it to get below boiling heat. Serve with hot pudding sauce.—Mrs. J E. Bratt.

AMERICAN PLUM PUDDING

1 cup suet shredded and chopped fine in flour
⅔ cup New Orleans Molasses and sugar
1 cup sour milk
1 cup currants
1 teaspoon soda

2 teaspoons cinnamon
½ teaspoon salt
½ teaspoon nutmeg

2 eggs

Make a little more stiff than cake batter, steam 3 hours.

SAUCE FOR PUDDING

1 cup water
½ cup brown sugar
1 egg beaten light

2 tablespoons butter
1 tablespoon vinegar
½ teaspoon cinnamon

2 tablespoons flour

Boil together.—Mrs. J. E. Hulbish.

CHERRY PUDDING

1 quart red cherries   3 tablespoons cornstarch

Heat cherries, and add cornstarch mixed with a little of the cold juice of the cherries. Cook until thoroughly heated, turn into wet mold and set aside to harden and chill. Serve with whipped cream or ice cream. This should be made 4 or 5 hours before using.—Mrs. A. F. Grenell.

CRANBERRY PUDDING

1 pint of cranberries   1 pint of flour
½ teaspoon of salt   · 2 teaspoons baking powder
¾ cup of milk

Mix and steam 1 hour.

SAUCE FOR SAME
1 cup sugar   ·   1½ tablespoons butter
2 eggs

Beat all together and add 1 cup of boiling milk. Cook until it thickens slightly.—Mrs. Wm. H. Moore.

LEMON PUDDING

PART I
1 large lemon   1 tablespoon butter
1 cup sugar   2 cups water

PART II
½ cup of sugar   ½ cup of milk
1 tablespoon of butter   ½ cup of flour
1 egg   2 teaspoons baking powder

Slice lemon very thin, add to rest of Part 1 and cook until lemon is done Cream butter and sugar of Part 2, add egg and then alternately milk and flour sifted with baking powder. Put this batter in buttered baking dish, pour into it the boiling syrup. Bake 30 minutes.—E. B. H. Thompson (Mrs. E. A. T.)

APPLE PUDDING

Have a baking dish well greased; fill ¾ full with apples, sliced; sprinkle with sugar as needed, cinnamon or nutmeg; add a little water.

BATTER
½ cup sugar   Pinch of salt
1 egg   ½ cup milk
1 teaspoon butter   ⅛ cup flour
⅞ teaspoon baking powder

Mix thoroughly, pour over apples, bake slowly until apples are done. Serve with sauce.—Mrs. F. J. Lewis.

Good Recipes

(1906)

————◆◆◆————

Good Recipes was published by the Woman's Society of the Winnetka Congregational Church of Winnetka, Illinois, in 1906. The church was founded in 1874 by a non-denominational body of 22 souls. From its beginning, the church confirmed the unity of its faith through a congregation which at one time encompassed 37 different denominations. It stressed involvement in and service to its community and beyond. A generation before women won their suffrage, they voted on a community issue in a church-held meeting, exercising the right to vote perhaps for the first time in American history. The third home of the church took the form of a Norman-style stone structure on Lincoln Avenue. It is now known as the Children's Chapel and is located at 725 Pine St.

GOOD RECIPES

"Nothing lovelier can be found in woman than to study household good."—MILTON.

PUBLISHED BY THE WOMAN'S SOCIETY OF THE
WINNETKA CONGREGATIONAL CHURCH
WINNETKA, ILLINOIS

Pea Soup

Pick over and wash 1 quart of dried peas, and soak over night in 3 quarts of cold water. In the morning pour off all this water, put the peas into the soup kettle with 7 quarts of cold water, 1 pound of salt pork, 3 cloves, 2 large onions, and 1 teaspoonful of celery salt. Boil gently for seven hours, stirring often, and at the end of that time rub the soup through a fine sieve. Return it to the kettle and add 2 bay leaves and 2 sprigs of parsley tied together. Add a pint of milk or cream, and after the soup boils up serve with toasted bread cut into dice.   Mrs. Rudolph Matz.

Pea Soup with Rice

Boil 1 teaspoonful of rice. Cook until tender 1 pint or 1 can of peas. Add to the rice and peas 1 pint of hot water and let boil, then remove from the fire and stir in quickly the yolk of 1 egg, beaten with 1 pint of cream. Salt and pepper to taste. This may or may not be rubbed through a colander.   Mrs. Frank Bissell.

Mock Bisque Soup

One half can of tomatoes, 1 teaspoonful of corn starch, 1 quart of milk, 1 teaspoonful of salt, $\frac{1}{3}$ cup of butter, $\frac{1}{2}$ salt spoonful of pepper. Stew the tomatoes until soft enough to strain easily. Boil the milk in a double boiler. Cook 1 teaspoonful of the butter and the cornstarch together in a small saucepan, adding enough of the hot milk to make it pour easily. Stir it carefully into boiling milk and boil ten minutes. Add the remainder of the butter in small pieces and stir until well mixed. Add salt and pepper and the strained tomatoes. If the tomatoes be very acid, add $\frac{1}{2}$ salt spoonful of soda before straining. Serve very hot.

Mrs. C. C. Blatchford.

Cheese Souffle

2 tablespoons butter, ½ teaspoon salt, 1 heaping tablespoonful flour, dash of cayenne, ½ cupful of milk, 3 eggs, 1 cupful grated cheese. Put the butter into a saucepan; when it is melted, stir in the flour and let it cook a minute (but not color), stirring all the time; add one half cupful of milk slowly and stir till smooth, then add salt and cayenne. Remove from the fire and add, stirring constantly, the beaten yolks of three eggs and the cupful of grated American or Parmesan cheese. Replace it on the fire, and stir until the cheese is melted and the paste smooth and consistent (do not cook too long, or the butter will separate). Pour the mixture on a butter dish and set away to cool. When ready to use, stir into it lightly the well-beaten whites of the three eggs; turn it into a pudding dish and bake in a hot oven for twenty to thirty minutes. Do not open the oven door for ten minutes; do not slam the oven door; do not move the souffle until after fifteen minutes; serve it at once when done. Like any souffle, it must go directly from the oven to the table, or it will fall.

Mrs. Morris Greeley.

Baked Beans Recipe

Wash the beans and soak them over night. Boil them slowly until tender, changing the water several times. Boil with them a small piece of salt pork, a bay leaf, and an onion. Remove them from the water when the skin will break easily; put them in a bean-pot, bury in them ½ lb. salt pork, with rind scored; sprinkle with salt and pepper. Pour over them a tablespoonful of molasses and enough salted water to cover them. Cover the pot closely and place it in a slow oven to cook for six to eight hours.

Mrs. Morris Greeley.

Meat Loaf

Three pounds lean meat chopped fine, 2 eggs, 8 crackers rolled, Kenosha or Boston, ½ small cup water, 1 tablespoon salt, 1 small tablespoon pepper, 1 nutmeg. Mix thoroughly, bake slowly one and a half hours.   Mrs. Jesse B. Alton.

Croquettes

One pint milk, scalded; 2 level teaspoonfuls butter, 4 heaping tablespoonfuls flour or 2 of cornstarch, ½ teaspoonful salt, ½ teaspoonful celery salt, ½ salt spoon white pepper, trifle of cayenne. Place the butter in a granite saucepan, and when it bubbles add the flour or cornstarch and stir until well mixed. To this add ⅓ of the hot milk and stir as it boils and thickens; then add ½ of the remainder and bring again to a boil, and when perfectly smooth add the rest of the milk. It should be very thick when done, almost like drop batter. Stir in the salt, celery salt, and pepper. Mix in while hot with the fish or meat which has already been seasoned. If more highly seasoned sauce is desired use ½ a sliced onion, 3 sprigs of parsley, 2 allspice, and scald with the milk. A stalk of celery may be cooked in the milk instead of the celery salt.   Mrs. R. M. Graves.

Muskmelon Pickle

Choose small, hard melons, which will not ripen; pare and slice. To each 10 pounds allow 3½ pounds granulated sugar, 3 pints cider vinegar, a good handful of whole cinnamon, some cloves and allspice. Boil twenty minutes, dip out spice and pour hot over the melon. Repeat after twenty-four hours. The third morning cook the melon in the liquor until tender, dip out, and boil the liquor and spice down to a thick syrup, remove most of the spice and turn syrup over the melon.   Mame McFarlin.

Oil Pickle

Twelve cucumbers sliced thin without peeling; 6 onions sliced. Put ½ cup salt on both and let stand for 2 hours. Drain and rinse with cold water and then add, 1 pint vinegar, ½ cup white mustard seed, ½ cup black mustard seed, 2 tablespoons celery seed. Put in glass jars. When serving add olive oil to taste.

Mrs. Landon Hoyt.

Tomato Soy for Cold Meats

One peck ripe tomatoes, peeled; 4 green peppers, 4 large onions. Chop and boil all together for one hour. Add ½ teacup salt, 2 teaspoonfuls cinnamon, 2 teaspoonfuls cloves, 2 cups sugar, 1 small teaspoonful black pepper. Let boil hard, then add one quart vinegar and take immediately from fire; seal while hot.

Belle W. Thorne.

Strawberry Jelly

One and a half pint berries, after they are washed and capped; 1 pint sugar, ¼ cup water. Boil sugar and water until it threads, then add berries and boil twenty minutes. This will make five glasses of jelly.   Catherine C. Poarch.

Graham Pudding

One cup molasses, 1 cup milk, 1 even teaspoon soda, 1½ cups Graham flour, 1 cup raisins, 1 small teaspoon cinnamon, ½ nutmeg, ½ teaspoon of salt. Piece of butter size of walnut. Put butter in pan it is cooked in. Steam three hours. Sauce, yolk of 1 egg, 1 cup sugar.   Mrs. J. B. Alton.

Brown Betty Pudding

Spread in the bottom of a baking dish a layer of bread crumbs and scatter bits of butter over them. Cover this with a layer of sliced or chopped apples, sprinkled with sugar and cinnamon. Over this spread another layer of the bread crumbs, and so proceed until the dish is full, the last layer being of crumbs and butter. Lastly, pour in around the edges 1 cup of hot water. Cover until the apples are nearly cooked, and then leave brown on top. Eat with sugar and cream.   Jane E. Dale.

Cranberry Pudding

Half cup butter, 1 cup sugar, 3 eggs, 3½ cups flour, 1¼ tablespoons baking powder, ½ cup milk, 1½ cups cranberries. Cream the butter, add sugar gradually, and eggs well beaten. Mix and sift flour and baking powder, and add alternately with milk to first mixture, stir in berries previously washed, turn into buttered gem pans and bake twenty-five minutes. Serve with Foamy Sauce.

Foamy Sauce

Two eggs, whites; 1 cup pulverized sugar, ½ cup butter, juice of ⅓ lemon. Cream butter, add sugar gradually, and the lemon juice. Just before serving add whites, stiffly beaten.

Inez M. Cutter.

Suet Pudding

One cup finely chopped suet, 1 cup molasses, 1 cup milk, 3 cups flour, 1 teaspoon soda, ½ teaspoon salt, ½ cup chopped raisins, ½ cup currants, ½ teaspoon each ginger, cloves and nutmeg; 1 teaspoon cinnamon. Mix and sift dry ingredients, add molasses and milk to suet, combine mixtures, add chopped fruit. Turn into buttered molds, cover and steam three hours. This makes four baking powder tins full. Serve with egg sauce.

Egg Sauce

One cup sugar, 1 egg, 1 lemon, juice and grated rind. Beat egg and sugar together until light, add ½ pint boiling water, let come to a boil, remove from fire and add lemon juice and rind.

Mrs. E. J. Allsebrooke.

Apple Tapioca Pudding

Three-fourths pearl tapioca, soaked over night in 1 quart of water. Cook in double boiler until clear and will pour like cream. Add ¾ cup sugar, a small piece of butter, a little nutmeg, and salt. Mix well together and pour into a baking dish, which has been buttered and half filled with sliced apples. Bake and serve with cream.

Jane E. Dale.

English Plum Pudding

One pound suet, 1 pound raisins, 1 pound currants, ¾ pound soda crackers, ¼ pound citron and small piece of candied lemon peel, 1 pound brown sugar, 1 teaspoon salt, 1 tablespoon molasses, 1 pint milk, 6 eggs, spices to suit. Figs and nuts may be added if desired, also wineglass of brandy. Put in molds and steam five hours.

Mrs. C. S. Thorne.

English Cherry Pie

One cup lard and butter mixed, 2 cups flour, 1 teaspoon salt. Work the shortening into the flour with a knife, mix with sufficient ice water to hold together, handling as little as possible.   Line the sides of a deep earthen baking dish, fill two-thirds full with stoned cherries, add two cups sugar and place 1 small cup (inverted) in the center of the dish.   Cover with a thick top crust, no bottom crust being used.   Spread over the crust a liberal coating of lard or butter before placing in oven.   Mrs. C. S. Thorne.

Lemon Pie

One lemon (grate rind and juice) 1 cup cold water, 1 cup sugar, 1 large tablespoon cornstarch, butter size of walnut, 3 eggs.   Put water, sugar and cornstarch on fire and stir until thick, adding yolks and lemon last, pour into crust which has been previously baked, and spread whites of eggs beaten stiff, and sweetened to taste, over top and brown slightly.   Lilian L. Cole.

Squash or Pumpkin Pie

Mix 1 cupful each of milk and dry steamed pumpkin, ½ cupful sugar, 2 tablespoonfuls each of molasses and melted butter, one teaspoonful of ginger, 2 eggs slightly beaten, 1 teaspoonful cinnamon and ½ teaspoonful of salt.   Pour into a pastry-lined plate and bake in a moderate oven for forty-five minutes.

Lilian L. Cole.

Apple Custard Pie

1 pint of sweet milk, 3 grated sweet apples, 2 well beaten eggs, a little salt, and sugar and nutmeg to taste.   Bake with under crust only.

Othello Cake

One cup sugar, $\frac{1}{2}$ cup butter, $\frac{1}{2}$ cup milk, 1 oz. chocolate, $\frac{1}{2}$ teaspoon vanilla, 1$\frac{3}{4}$ cups flour, 1 teaspoon baking powder, 2 whites of eggs, 4 yolks. Scrape chocolate, add 3 teaspoons of the sugar, and 1 teaspoon water, stir over fire till smooth. Add with vanilla, to creamed butter and sugar. Add beaten yolks, beaten in flour sifted with baking powder, then beaten whites. Bake in layers or in one cake, as preferred. Frosting: Beat 2 cups powdered sugar into 2 whites, add 2 ozs. melted chocolate, 1 teaspoon vanilla, and 1 pint chopped walnut meats. This is enough for a four-layer cake.   Mrs. B. S. Winchester.

Coffee Cake

One cup sugar, $\frac{1}{2}$ cup molasses, $\frac{1}{2}$ cup butter, $\frac{1}{2}$ cup cold coffee, 2$\frac{1}{4}$ cups flour, 2 eggs, 1 teaspoonful soda, 1 teaspoonful cloves, 1 teaspoonful cinnamon, 1 cup raisins, $\frac{1}{2}$ cup currants, $\frac{1}{4}$ pound citron. Dissolve soda in coffee.

Sponge Cake

Weigh 10 eggs; allow their weight in flour. Beat the yolks light, whip the sugar into them, stir in half the grated peel and all the juice of a lemon, then the flour, lastly the whites folded in lightly. Bake in a loaf tin in a very steady oven.

Mrs. J. O. Parker.

Sponge Cake

Yolks of 3 eggs beaten light, 1 cup sugar, 3 tablespoons hot water. Add 1 level cup flour into which 1 teaspoon baking powder has been sifted. Flavor, then fold lightly in the whites of the eggs, which have been beaten stiff. Bake in little cake tins in a quick oven.   Mrs. C. Prouty.

Ginger Drop Cakes

One-fourth cup butter or drippings, ½ cup sugar, 1 cup molasses, 2 eggs, 1 teaspoon each ginger and cloves, 1 cup boiling water, 2 teaspoons soda, mixed with little salt, 2½ cups flour. Cream butter, add sugar and eggs, well beaten, the molasses and boiling water. Sift soda and salt with flour, add to first mixture with the spices. Beat well, and bake in greased and floured gem pans about fifteen minutes. This makes twenty cakes. Sift powdered sugar over tops after baking.   Inez M. Cutter.

Fairy Gingerbread

One-half cup butter, 1 cup sugar, ½ cup milk, 1⅞ cups flour. Cream butter, add sugar gradually and milk very slowly. Mix and sift flour and ginger and combine mixture. Spread very thinly with a broad-bladed knife on a buttered inverted dripping pan. Bake in moderate oven. Cut in squares before removing from pan.   Mrs. McCordic.

Margerettes

White of 1 egg, well beaten, ½ cup powdered sugar, ½ teaspoon baking powder, ½ cup English walnuts or pecans ground or chopped fine. Stir all together, spread on Long Branch crackers, set in a slow oven until a slight tinge of brown is seen on the mixture. Nice with tea or as cake with dessert. Caroline C. Poarch.

Rocks

One and one-half cups of sugar, 1 cup of butter, 1½ cups raisins, 1 cup of chopped nuts, 3 cups of flour, 4 eggs, 1 teaspoon soda, 1 teaspoon cinnamon, pinch of salt. Drop from spoon on buttered tin.   Mrs. Landon Hoyt.

FOR THE CHAFING-DISH

"Man is an animal that cooks his victuals."—BURKE.

Capilotade of Turkey

Cut up the remains of cold turkey in small pieces. Put in the chafing dish 2 tablespoons of butter, and when melted add 2 tablespoons of flour, stirring constantly until smooth; season with pepper, salt and 1 tablespoon of chopped parsley. Add ½ pint of cream or milk, put in the turkey with ½ can of mushrooms. Let it simmer for ten minutes, then add 1 glass of sherry and serve on small squares of toast. Mrs. W. C. Boyden.

Welsh Rarebit

One half pound cheese, 2 eggs, trifle cayenne pepper, 1 teaspoonful mustard, ½ teaspoonful salt, 1 tablespoon butter, ½ cup cream. Break the cheese into small pieces and put with the other ingredients into the chafing dish. Stir until the cheese melts, then spread on slices of crisp toast and serve immediately.

Jane E. Dale.

Finnan Haddie

(*Armour Institute.*)

The fish — a thick one — simmer in water, cold at beginning, ten minutes; after draining pick in pieces.

Cream Sauce

One tablespoon butter, 1 tablespoon flour, 1 cup cream. Season, salt, cayenne pepper, 2 teaspoons lemon juice. Add fish, heat thoroughly, serve on toast or with potatoes.

FOR THE SICK-ROOM

*"Now, good digestion wait on appetite, and health
on both!"*—SHAKESPEARE.

Buttermilk Gruel

One pint cold buttermilk, 2 eggs well beaten.   Mix thoroughly
and bring to a boil, stirring constantly.   Sweeten and flavor to
taste.   A pleasant drink for the sick-room.   Jane E. Dale.

Lemon Foam

(Passavant Hospital.   Individual for convalescents.)

Two eggs, 2 tablespoons sugar, juice and grated rind of ½
lemon.   Beat yolks in sugar, add lemon, and put bowl in dish
of boiling water over fire.   Stir until mixture begins to thicken,
add beaten whites and stir 2 two minutes, or until whole is like
thick cream.   Remove from fire and serve quite cold in cups or
glasses.   Mrs. B. S. Winchester.

Mutton Broth

A 2 pound shank of mutton (do not get the rib); wash, put
in two quarts of hot water; boil until the meat drops from the
bones — sometimes three hours — add water as needed, then
remove the meat, set the liquor away to cool; when cold, lift the
fat from the liquor and if any particles of fat are left, take them
off; then put liquor on to boil, add a pinch of salt, boil down to
about 1 quart; strain; if not salt enough, add salt and pepper
when served; good either hot or cold.

Boston Brown Bread

One pint of rye or graham flour, 1 pint corn meal scalded in ⅓ quart boiling water, ⅓ quart sour milk, a little salt, 1 small cup molasses, 1 rounded teaspoonful soda dissolved in water. Steam four hours and dry in oven.   Mrs. S. W. Crandall.

Updated Version
Makes one loaf

Ingredients:
1 cup all-purpose flour
2 cups whole wheat flour
1 teaspoon salt
2 teaspoons baking soda
2/3 cup firmly packed brown sugar
½ cup chopped walnuts
½ raisins (can substitute Craisins)
¼ cup molasses
2 cups buttermilk

Directions:
Preheat oven to 350 degrees. Mix together the flours, salt, baking soda, brown sugar, walnuts, and raisins. Add molasses and buttermilk and mix until moist. Pour the batter into a greased and floured 9 x 5 loaf pan and bake for one hour, or until a knife comes out clean.

How We Cook
in Los Angeles
(1894)

———◆———

How We Cook in Los Angeles was published by the Ladies Social Circle of the Simpson M. E. Church of Los Angeles, California, in 1894. This church no longer stands.

The book is notable for its lengthy Preface, written by Jessie Ann Benton Frémont (May 31, 1824–December 27, 1902), a great American writer and political activist, which captures the spirit of cooking and entertaining of its time. Frémont's initial notability came from her family: she was the daughter of Missouri Senator Thomas Hart Benton and the wife of military officer, explorer, and politician, John C. Frémont. She wrote many stories that were printed in popular magazines of the time as well as several books of historical value. Her writings, which helped support her family during times of financial difficulty, were memoirs of her husband's, and her own, time in the American West—back when the West was an exotic frontier.

A great supporter of her husband, who was one of the first two Senators of the new U.S. state of California and a Governor of the Territory of Arizona, she was outspoken on political issues and a determined opponent of slavery, which was excluded from the formation of California. By maintaining a high level of political involvement during a period that was extremely unfavorable for women, Jessie Benton Frémont proved herself to be years ahead of her time.

HOW WE COOK

IN

LOS ANGELES

A Practical Cook-Book Containing Six Hundred or
More Recipes Selected and Tested by
over Two Hundred Well
Known Hostesses

Including a French, German and Spanish Department

With Menus,

Suggestions for Artistic Table Decorations,
and Souvenirs

BY THE

Ladies' Social Circle, Simpson M. E. Church

LOS ANGELES, CAL.

"*Some ha'e meat that canna' eat,
And some wad eat that want it,
But we ha'e meat and we can eat,
And sae the Lord be thankit.*"

LOS ANGELES, CAL
COMMERCIAL PRINTING HOUSE
mdcccxciv.

CHICKEN SALAD
Mrs. E. A. Otis.

In mixing chicken salad allow one yolk of an egg to each chicken, and to four chickens one and a half pints of olive oil. Pick the chickens apart with fingers, removing carefully all fat and skin. Then take celery, pick likewise into small pieces and add it to the chicken until there is an equal quantity of each. If celery cannot be obtained, use lettuce prepared in the same manner.

For the dressing one level teaspoon of salt to each yolk of an egg; pepper to taste, one teaspoon of dry mustard, and juice of one lemon, more if the lemon is not very juicy. The oil should be added a few drops at a time, stirring constantly. While stirring, add an occasional drop of vinegar. To this mixture add the last thing one-half cup of rich cream, and when thoroughly mixed, pour over the salad just before it is served. The object of the lemon is to cut the oil, and make the dressing of a cream-like consistency.

SALAD OF STUFFED EGGS
Mrs. L. J. Rose.

One dozen eggs; 2 tablespoons Howland's olive oil; onions, salt, red pepper.

Peel and cut in halves the hard-boiled eggs; remove the yolks, mash and add the oil. Use a little onion, salt and pepper to taste; when thoroughly mixed, fill the white cups. Press them together and serve on lettuce leaves.

EGG SALAD
Mrs. J. A. Fairchild.

Six hard-boiled eggs; 3 medium-sized pickles; 1 teaspoon mustard; 2 teaspoons sugar; 1 teaspoon salt; 1 tablespoon Howland's olive oil; 2 tablespoons vinegar; a little parsley, a little pepper.

Cut the eggs in halves; take out the yolks, powder them, and mix with the chopped pickles, parsley, and other seasoning. Cut a small piece from the round end of the eggs; fill with the mixture, and garnish with parsley.

TOMATO CREAM SOUP
Miss M. E. McLellan.

Six tomatoes; 1 small salt spoon soda; 1 pint of milk; 2 large teaspoons flour; 1 dessertspoon butter.

Stew the tomatoes, add the soda, then strain through a fine strainer. Boil the milk and thicken it with the flour; add the butter, then the tomato. Season to taste and serve.

TOMATO SOUP
Mrs. A. C. St. John.

One pint cooked tomatoes; 1 teaspoon salt; pinch of soda; 3 rolled crackers; ¼ teaspoon pepper: 1 heaping tablespoon butter; 1 quart sweet milk.

Put the tomatoes through a sieve, add the soda and boil for five minutes; then add the milk, butter, salt and pepper; when this boils add the rolled crackers; let just boil and serve at once.

Instead of the quart of milk, a pint of water and a pint of milk may be used, and still make an excellent soup.

GREEN PEA SOUP
Mrs. J. Wigmore.

Three pints green peas; ¼ pound of butter: 2 slices ham; 3 onions, sliced; 4 heads lettuce, (shredded); 2 French rolls, (crumbs of); 2 handfuls spinach; 1 lump sugar; 2 quarts medium stock.

Put the butter, ham, 1 quart peas, onions and lettuce to a pint of stock; simmer one hour; add the rest of the stock and the rolled crumbs; boil for another hour. Boil the spinach and squeeze dry. Rub the soup through a sieve, and spinach with it to color it. Then have ready 1 pint of young peas boiled, add them to the soup. Put in sugar, give one boil and serve.

GREEN PEA SOUP.
Mrs. Edward Silent.

One quart green peas; 1 quart water; 1 pint milk; ½ teaspoon salt; ¼ saltspoon pepper: ½ teaspoon sugar; 1 table spoon butter: 1 tablespoon flour.

Put the peas into 1 pint of boiling water and cook until soft.   Mash them in the water in which they boiled, and rub through a strainer, gradually adding a pint of water.   Put on to boil again   Cook the butter and flour in a small sauce pan, being careful not to brown it.   Stir into the boiling soup. Add salt, pepper, sugar and the milk, which should be hot.

This is a good way to use cold peas, or peas that are old and hard.   When the pods are fresh, wash them thoroughly, allow more water, and cook them with the peas.

BEAN SOUP

"76."

One quart small white beans; 1 quart cold water, (to be thrown away after five minutes boiling); 1 scant teaspoon soda; 2 quarts rich milk; 2 quarts cold water; salt and but-ter to taste.

Boil beans in 1 quart of water with the soda five minutes; take out, throw away water, and rub skins off in cold water; then put beans into 2 quarts of cold water and boil until very soft; this will require 2 or 3 hours.   Add the milk, pepper, salt and butter to taste; boil up once, and it is ready to serve. This is a superior soup.

CELERY SOUP

Mrs. A. S. Averill.

Bones of a roasted turkey or chicken; 3 good heads celery; butter and milk.

Take the bones of a roasted turkey or chicken with the bits not suitable for reappearance upon the table, cover with cold water, and boil thoroughly two or three hours.   Strain out the bones and set aside for stock.

Cut up the celery, using all not fit for table.   Cover with hot water, and boil until soft.   Strain through colander.   Add stock and season.   Add butter and sufficient good rich milk. Serve hot.

BROILED OYSTERS

"76."

Finely rolled crackers; some melted butter; salt.

The oysters, after being strained, are rolled in cracker crumbs; then shaken gently on a rough towel. Dip in melted butter; roll in cracker crumbs and broil on gridiron. Serve hot.

CURRIED OYSTERS

Practical Housekeeping.

One quart of oysters; ½ cup of butter; 2 tablespoons flour; 1 tablespoon curry powder.

Drain the liquid from the oysters into a sauce pan, add butter, flour, and curry powder well mixed. Boil; add oysters and a little salt. Boil up once, and serve.

OYSTER ROLL

Cut a round piece of bread six inches across, from the top of a well-baked round loaf. Remove the inside, leaving a crust half an inch thick. Make a rich oyster stew, put in the crust first a layer of the oysters; then of bread crumbs. Repeat until it is filled. Put the cover on top. Glaze the loaf with the beaten yolk of an egg. Place in the oven for a few moments. Serve very hot.

OYSTER PIE

Two pounds of veal; 1 quart of oysters; suet, flour, butter, salt, pepper, biscuit dough.

Cut the veal, and a small piece of suet into small pieces. Boil until well done. Thicken the stock with flour, remove from the fire, add oysters, some bits of butter, pepper, and salt. Place in buttered baking dish and cover with a crust, prepared as for baking powder biscuit. Bake until the crust is done.

OYSTER PATTIES

Mrs. A. C. St. John.

Pie crust; oysters; butter; pepper, salt.

Line gem pans with rich pie crust, and bake in a quick

oven. Have ready a stew made of either canned, or fresh oysters, quite thick, and well seasoned. Remove the crusts from the pans, fill with the oysters, and serve hot. These with baked potatoes are good for luncheon.

One pint of oysters makes one dozen patties.

OYSTER SHORT CAKE
Mrs. Susie G. Hill.

One and a half cups flour; 1 tablespoon lard; ½ teaspoon Cleveland's baking powder; a pinch of salt; sweet milk; butter size of an egg.

Mix baking powder, salt and lard in the dry flour; add just enough milk to make a dough that will roll out. Spread on butter, roll it again, and repeat until all the butter is used. Bake in two layers in a quick oven.

Filling—1 quart of oysters; 1 tablespoon butter; ½ cup of sweet milk; 3 crackers, salt, pepper.

Season the oysters with butter, salt and pepper. Stew them a few minutes, add the milk, and when it comes to the boiling point, add the cracker, finely rolled. Place between and on top of the cake.

OYSTER COCKTAIL
Miss Ruth Childs.

Three tablespoons of tomato catsup; 6 tablespoons oyster liquor; 2 teaspoons Worcestershire sauce; 2 teaspoons pepper sauce; 3 lemons, juice only; a little salt; 175 California oysters. Mix and serve.

OYSTERS IN ICE
Mrs. Hugh W. Vail.

Take a block of ice one-and-a-half feet long by one foot wide. Melt the center with a plate full of hot water. Place several oysters in the hollow, and slices of lemon around the top. Set the ice on a napkin, and garnish with watercress, or parsley.

TONGUE CROQUETTES
Mrs. J. H. Norton.

One tongue, good size; 2 eggs, beaten; small quantity potatoes, cooked; melted butter; Worcestershire sauce, celery salt, salt, pepper.

Boil the tongue very tender, chop very fine.   Add the potatoes chopped, the eggs and a small quantity of melted butter; season.   Make into any shape desired. Roll in beaten egg, then in cracker dust, fry in hot lard to a light brown. Garnish with green and serve.

SHAD ROE CROQUETTES
Miss Parloa.

One pint cream; 4 tablespoons corn starch; 4 shad roe; 4 tablespoons butter; 1 teaspoon salt; the juice of two lemons; a slight grating of nutmeg, and a speck of cayenne.

Boil the roe fifteen minutes in salted water, then drain, and mash.   Put the cream on to boil.   Mix the butter and cornstarch together, and stir into the boiling cream.   Add the seasoning and roe. Boil up once, and set away to cool. Shape, and fry.

OYSTER CROQUETTES

One can oysters; 1 set brains; 1 egg; bread crumbs, parsley, butter, salt, cracker crumbs, cayenne pepper.

Dry the oysters, chop them fine; add the brains and enough bread crumbs to mold; add the beaten egg, a little butter, the parsley chopped, cayenne and salt. Make in shapes, roll in cracker crumbs and fry.

POTATO CROQUETTES
Mrs. Alice Curtain.

Four or five potatoes; butter and cream; 1 egg; cracker crumbs; oil or lard; salt.

Boil and mash thoroughly the potatoes, season to taste with butter, salt, and cream.   Beat to a cream, then add the well-beaten white of the egg.   Make into rolls, dip into the beaten yolk of the egg, then into cracker crumbs.   Put into a wire basket and fry in deep hot lard until brown.

CHICKEN 'a la MERINGO

Mrs. C. H. Walton.

Two chickens; salt pork; 2 tablespoons of butter; 2 table-spoons of onions; 4 tablespoons of flour; 1 quart white stock or water; 1 cup of strained tomato; 1 cup of mushrooms; olives.

Singe and cut up the chickens. Roll the pieces in flour and fry them brown in pork fat. Brown the onions in the butter, add flour and stock, simmer five minutes; season; add the tomato, pour over the chicken. Cook twenty minutes. Add mushrooms and olives.

JELLIED CHICKEN

Mrs. W. G. Whorton.

One chicken; 2 tablespoons gelatine; hard-boiled eggs; salt; pepper.

Boil the chicken in as little water as possible until the meat falls from the bones, chop fine; season with salt and pepper. Put in a mold a layer of chicken, then a layer of sliced eggs; alternate these until the mold is nearly full; Boil down to one half the liquor which is left in the pot. While warm, add the gelatine; when dissolved, pour over the chicken. Set in a cool place to jelly.

PRESSED CHICKEN

Mrs. J. W. Gillette.

Two chickens; 1 cup of butter; 1 tablespoon of salt; 1 teaspoon of pepper; 1 beaten egg; a little parsley; hard-boiled eggs.

Boil the chickens until the meat separates from the bones. Chop the meat. Boil the liquor until it is reduced to a cupful. Add to this the butter, salt, pepper, parsley and beaten egg. Stir this mixture into the chicken. Lay slices of boiled egg in a dish, press in the chicken. Serve, garnished with celery tops.

ROAST WILD DUCK

Mrs. W. G. W.

Before roasting, parboil them, with a small peeled carrot placed in each; this will absorb the fishy flavor which most wild ducks have. When parboiled, throw away the carrots, and lay the ducks in fresh water half an hour. Dry, and stuff with bread crumbs seasoned with pepper, salt and sage (or onion.) Roast until brown and tender, basting alternately with butter and water, and the drippings. When the ducks are taken up, add a teaspoon of currant jelly and a pinch of cayenne pepper to the gravy; thicken with browned flour, and serve in a tureen.

FRIED RABBIT

Mrs. J. W. Hendricks.

A young cottontail rabbit; bacon; flour; hot lard.

Soak the rabbit four or five hours in strong, salt water. Cut in pieces suitable for frying. Roll in flour, and drop into hot lard, to which two or three good-sized pieces of bacon have been added. Season well. Cook thoroughly and it will be as nice as chicken.

BARBECUED RABBIT

Two tablespoons vinegar; 1 tablespoon made mustard; pepper, salt, butter, parsley.

Clean and wash the rabbit; open it all the way on the under side. Lay it flat in salted water for half an hour. Wipe dry, and broil it, gashing the thick part of the back that the heat may penetrate it. When brown and tender, put it on a hot dish, add pepper, salt and butter; turning it over and over, that it may absorb the butter. Cover and set in the oven for five minutes. Heat the vinegar, and mustard; pour it over the rabbit; garnish with crisp parsley, and serve.

TO COOK A CALF'S HEAD
Mrs. T. B.

Tie the brains in muslin with sweet herbs.   Boil brains, head, haslet, and feet, two hours, adding the liver the last hour.   When nearly done take out the brains, and a portion of the lights.   Chop them with a hard boiled egg, season with salt, pepper, and a little butter, add a little of the broth; dredge lightly with flour and cook sufficiently to make a nice sauce.   Take up the rest of the meat, remove the bones, lay it on a dish, and pour the sauce over it.

SALT TONGUE
Miss Parloa.

Soak over night, and cook from five to six hours.   Throw into cold water and peel off the skin.

FRESH TONGUE
Miss Parloa.

Put into boiling water to cover, with two tablespoons of salt.   Cook from five to six hours.   Skin the same as salt tongue.

BREAKFAST FRITTERS
Mrs. W. W. Ross.

One cup minced meat; 1 cup sweet milk; 1 tablespoon bread crumbs; 1 tablespoon flour; egg, pepper, salt.

Mix and season.   Make into small cakes and fry them a light brown in deep fat.

MEAT CAKES
Mrs. S. J. Peck.

Three cups chopped meat; 1 cup mashed potato; 2 eggs, salt, pepper and sage.

To any cold meat chopped fine, add the potatoes, eggs and seasonings.   Work all together; form into cakes, roll in flour and fry.

ESCALOPED ONIONS
Mrs. Mondini Wood.

Onions; cracker crumbs; cream; butter; pepper; salt.

Cook thirty sliced onions in salted water until very tender (they will be more delicate if the water is changed.) Put a layer of onions in a baking dish, then a layer of crumbs seasoned with butter, pepper and salt. Repeat until the desired amount is prepared, finishing with the crackers. Add a little of the onion water and sufficient cream to make very moist. Bake until a light brown.

BOILED ONIONS

Remove the tops, roots and thin outer skin. Put them in cold water and parboil. Drain, and cook them very tender in plenty of milk and water, salted. Drain again and put them in a hot dish. Season with salt, pepper, and bits of butter.

STUFFED OLIVES
Mrs. T. A. Lewis.

Open olives, take out pits, and stuff with chopped truffles.

CREAMED PARSNIPS
H. F. G.

Parsnips; 2 tablespoons butter; pepper; salt; a little minced parsley; 3 tablespoons of cream; ¼ tablespoon of flour.

Boil the parsnips until tender. Scrape, and slice lengthwise. Put over the fire, the butter and other seasonings. Shake until the mixture boils, then add the cream, mixed with the flour, boil once, and pour over the parsnips.

PARSNIPS
Mrs. Alice Curtain.

Parsnips; 1 egg; salt; pepper; butter.

Peel the parsnips, cut thin and cook with a little water, until dry. Mash fine, and season with butter, pepper and salt; beat up the egg and mix with the parsnips while hot, then fry in butter, or beef drippings or a mixture of both, as you would potato croquettes. Excellent.

LYONNAISE POTATOES
H. F. G.

One quart cooked potatoes; 3 tablespoons butter; 1 table-spoon chopped onion; 1 tablespoon chopped parsley; salt; pepper.

Fry the onion in the butter until it is slightly browned, then add the sliced potatoes, well salted and peppered. When thoroughly heated, add the parsley, and cook two minutes.

The onions may be omitted.

SARATOGA POTATOES
Mrs. W. W. Widney.

Pare, and slice potatoes thin as possible, lay them in ice water for an hour. Then dry them on a cloth. Drop the slices, few at a time, in deep hot lard, or better still cottolene. Fry to a delicate brown. Take up with a skimmer, lay them on clean soft paper. Sprinkle with salt, and set them in the open oven, to preserve their crispness. Serve either hot or cold.

BOILED RICE
X. Y. Z.

Wash the rice, drain, and put in boiling salted water. Boil twelve minutes, drain, cover with a thickly folded towel, set in the oven, leaving the door open, and steam it until the grains are dry and bursting.

SUMMER SQUASH
Mrs. M. R. Sinsabaugh.

Young squash; egg; cracker crumbs; corn meal; salt; pepper; butter, and lard.

Select solid squash, that have not begun to form seed, cut them in slices a quarter of an inch in thickness, lay them in salt and water for a few minutes. Dip each slice into beaten egg, roll in fine cracker crumbs and Indian meal, well salted and peppered. Fry in hot olive oil, or butter and lard mixed. Fry briskly at first, afterwards more slowly until tender.

FRUIT FRITTERS
Mrs. C. C. McLean.

Two eggs, whites; 1 tablespoon flour; 1 tablespoon cold water; 1 tablespoon butter. or Howland's olive oil; apricots, peaches, and strawberries.

Make a batter with the beaten whites of the eggs, flour, cold water and butter or oil. Mix thoroughly before putting in the whites. Pare the apricots and peaches, and cut in quarters, strawberries used whole. Dip each piece of fruit into the batter, and drop into the boiling fat. Two minutes will cook them brown and crisp; then sugar them and serve hot.

FRUIT DUMPLINGS
Mrs. E. R. Smith.

One pint flour; fruit; a little salt; 2 teaspoons Cleveland's baking powder; milk to make a *very* soft dough.

Sift the salt, baking powder and flour together; mix with milk till very soft. Place in a steamer well greased cups. Put in each a spoonful of batter, then one of fruit. Cover with another of batter. Steam twenty minutes. Serve with whipped cream or lemon sauce.

PEACH ROLLS
Mrs. M. G. Moore.

Stew dried fruit; sweeten and flavor to taste. Make a good baking powder crust, roll very thin and spread with fruit, putting small pieces of butter on the fruit. Roll up and place in a deep pan. To 3 or 4 rolls add 1 cup sugar, and ½ cup butter, and pour over this hot water enough to cover. Bake ½ hour. Serve with sauce or cream and sugar.

BLACKBERRY MUSH
Mrs. M. G. Moore.

Two quarts ripe berries; 1½ pints boiling water; 1 pound sugar; 1 pint sifted flour.

To the berries add the boiling water and sugar; cook a few minutes, then stir in flour. Boil until the flour is cooked. Serve hot or cold, with sweet cream or hard sauce.

TOMATO SAUCE
Mrs. E. A. Pruess.

One tablespoon lard; ½ teaspoon flour; 4 large tomatoes, chopped; 2 small chilis, chopped. Cook all together until done.

STUFFED PEPPERS
Mrs. J. G. Downey.

One dozen large peppers; 1 onion; ½ cup grated corn; 1 cup meat or chicken; 1 tablespoon lard or butter.

Remove the seeds from the peppers, then throw them upon a bed of live coals, turning them constantly until they are of a light brown; then take them up, throw them into cold water, and remove the skins. Heat the lard or butter in a saucepan, and add the minced onion; when this is hot, add the tomato, and grated corn, with pepper and salt. Let it simmer fifteen minutes, stirring occasionally to prevent burning. Remove from the fire. Add the minced meat or chicken. (A small slice of ham or bacon improves the flavor.) Mix well, stuff the peppers, and fry a light brown.

Sauce for the peppers.—One spoon butter; 1 spoon flour; 1 onion; 1 tomato; green pepper; 2 apples.

Chop the pepper, slice the onion and tomato. Add a few raisins and olives, and sufficient water to make a sauce. Boil until the apples are soft. Put the peppers in this sauce. Simmer a moment, then serve.

GREEN PEPPERS
Spanish Lady.

Beefsteak; green peppers; tomatoes; eggs; apples; raisins; sugar; vinegar; onions; thyme; pepper; salt.

Roast the peppers on hot coals, remove the skins and stuff them.

Stuffing—Boil and chop a steak fine, as for hash, fry chopped onions, one green pepper, one tomato, a little thyme, vinegar, pepper and salt to taste. When stuffed, roll them in flour, dip in beaten egg, and fry in hot fat.

Gravy—Make gravy by frying onions, peppers, tomatoes, a few raisins; slices of apple, thyme, vinegar, and a little sugar.

CALF'S FEET

Mrs. C. Ducommun.

Boil the feet three hours in four quarts water, remove the large bones, split and lay them in a sauce pan. Mix a little flour with two ounces of butter. Add it with pepper, salt, mace, and a little vinegar, to two cups of the liquor in which the feet were boiled. Simmer this ten minutes, garnish with sliced lemon. Serve very hot. The remainder of the jelly may be used as jelly.

MEAT BALLS

Mrs. C. Ducommun.

Two pounds veal; ½ pound bacon; 3 eggs, whites; milk bread; salt; pepper; nutmeg; fine herbs; lemon peel.

Mince the veal and bacon very fine. Add all the other ingredients. Mix thoroughly. Form into balls the size of a walnut. Cook in boiling water. When done, they rise to the surface. Place on a platter, and pour over them a white sauce, made of butter and flour, seasoned with a few drops of vinegar.

FOIE ä le POULETTE

Mrs. C. Ducommun.

One calf's liver; 1 onion, good size; flour; butter· pepper; salt; broth; vinegar.

Cut the liver in thin slices, dredge with flour, mince the onion and fry it in butter, then the liver. Cook a little, then add the other articles, a few drops of vinegar, a piece of butter. Stir until well mixed and serve.

FRESH PEAS

Mrs. C. Ducommun.

Put the peas over a brisk fire, with a piece of butter and a teaspoon flour. Stir until the butter is melted and well mixed. Then add a little boiling water. Cook half an hour, then season with salt, very little pepper, and a little sugar if liked, and they are ready to serve.

INVALID COOKERY

GRAHAM GEMS
Mrs. T. F. McCamant.

Mix a batter of graham flour and water. Let it stand until sour, the same as for old-fashioned buckwheat cakes. When of the proper consistency, add a little melted suet or butter and salt. While your gem tins are heating, stir in thoroughly ½ teaspoon soda. Bake in a hot oven. The quantity of soda must necessarily be regulated by the sourness of the batter, it is not always alike. "Practice makes perfect."

GRAHAM PANCAKES
Mrs. T. F. McCamant.

Mix the same as for gems, only thinner and leave out the shortening. Sour milk may be used instead of water. A little sugar put in the batter will make the cakes brown nicer. Use the soda of course.

EGG LEMONADE

Beat the white of one fresh egg; the juice of one lemon and a teaspoon of sugar into a glass of water. Pleasant and nourishing for invalids.

BAKED MILK

Put ½ gallon milk in a jar, and cover closely with writing paper, tie over the mouth. Let it stand in a moderate oven 8 or 10 hours. It will then be like cream, and is excellent for invalids; consumptives especially.

REFRESHING DRINK

One ℔ ground flax-seed and 2 lemons boiled together in 4 quarts of water. When cool, sweeten to taste. Good for persons with weak lungs.

ESCALOPED SALMON

Mrs. Adolf Ekstein.

Bread crumbs; salmon; milk; flour; butter; pepper; salt.

Place in baking dish alternate layers of bread crumbs, and salmon picked to pieces. Thicken some milk with a little flour; season with butter, salt and pepper. Pour over the fish while hot. Bake till brown.

Updated Version
Serves 6

Ingredients:
2 cans salmon
¼ cup fresh dill, chopped
2 medium onions, chopped
1 cup celery, chopped
2 cloves garlic, minced
Salt and pepper to taste
2 eggs, lightly beaten
1½ cup milk
6 tablespoons butter
3 cups saltine crackers, crushed

Directions:
Preheat oven to 350 degrees. Drain the salmon and mix it with the next 7 ingredients. Melt 4 tablespoons of butter and add it to the salmon mixture, along with 2 cups of the crushed crackers. Press into a greased 9 x 13 casserole dish. Melt the remaining 2 tablespoons of butter and add 1 cup of cracker crumbs, then sprinkle this mixture over the casserole. Bake for 45 minutes.

My Mother's Cook Book

(1880)

———⋙⬩⬩⬧⬩⬩⬤———

My Mother's Cook Book was "Compiled by Ladies of St. Louis, and sold for the benefit of the Women's Christian Home" of St. Louis, Missouri. It was published in 1880.

The book's florid, politically incorrect Preface claims that food and cooks are both heaven-sent, and that women should read the book because "This book will render Divorce Courts an expensive luxury, instead of a social necessity. It is the housekeeper's Magna Charta. Her Emancipation Proclamation. It is the first eloquent muttering of the domestic revolution by which Ethiopia and Hibernia will be hurled from their throne, the Saxon race regain its supremacy, and those terrible kitchen mandates issued by Bridget and Dinah, before which the young wife was wont to tremble and turn pale, will be as powerless as the Pope's bull against the comet." If that were not enough to strike fear in one's lily-white, Protestant heart and get one to buy a copy, the recipes were good, too. Do you think Amanda Wingfield's mother had one on her kitchen counter?

MY MOTHER'S

COOK BOOK

COMPILED BY

LADIES OF ST. LOUIS,

AND SOLD FOR THE BENEFIT OF THE

WOMEN'S CHRISTIAN HOME.

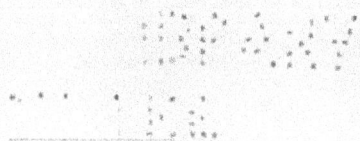

"Cookery is an Art,
Still changing and of momentary triumph;
Know, on thyself thy genius must depend;
All books of Cookery, all helps of Art,
Are vain, if void of genius thou wouldst cook."

SAINT LOUIS:
HUGH R. HILDRETH PRINTING COMPANY, 407 N. FOURTH STREET.
1880.

GUMBO SOUP.

Fry a knuckle of veal in butter, with pepper, salt and onions; after it is fried, add three dozen ochra, skinned, with the ends cut off, and a piece of ham. Pour two gallons of boiling water on this; when about half cooked, add four crabs; first boil them and divide each in four parts, frying them brown, with butter, pepper and salt. About two hours before dinner, add one dozen tomatoes, with the skins taken off.

GUMBO SOUP.

Fry five or six slices of salt-pork; after they are done, fry six large onions in the same fat; cut up and fry a good sized chicken; put these into a large pot with a small piece of lean ham and two quarts of water; when it boils put in one quart of sliced gumbo and the corn cut from two ears, a few tomatoes if you like, and a small piece of red pepper, no salt. Keep adding boiling water as it boils away. It should be on the fire five or six hours.

MISS EMILY TUCKER.

GUMBO SOUP.

Fry one large chicken or a knuckle of veal with two or three onions in a little lard until brown, put them in a soup kettle with a quart of gumbo sliced fine, and a quart of tomatoes previously peeled and sliced; add a gallon and a half of water, half a red pepper; boil slowly four or five hours and stir frequently with a wooden spoon.

MRS. C. B. RICHARDS.

MOCK OYSTER SOUP.

One pint tomatoes, well stewed; one quart boiling water; put in a teaspoonful of soda; when it has done foaming add one quart boiling milk; a piece of butter, size of an egg. Salt and pepper to taste. Pour upon three soda crackers rolled.

MRS. SAM'L COPP.

PILAF—TURKISH DISH.

Prepare a rich beef soup; season with tomatoes, pepper and salt; and while it is boiling add about half the quantity of rice, well washed; let the two boil together twenty minutes, or until the soup is entirely absorbed by the rice. Melt quickly half a pound of best butter, mix immediately with the rice, and serve in five minutes. If desired to have meat in the Pilaf, take either chicken, turkey, or lamb, roasted, cut in small pieces, and put it in the rice while boiling, ten minutes before taking from the fire, and before putting on the butter.   MRS. JASIGI.

TURTLE SOUP.

You must have the turtle alive; cut the head off and let it bleed to death.   Boil the turtle till the shells can be separated, and the meat is cooked.   Take off the gall bladder, and if you find a black ball (if there is any) throw it away.   Put butter and flour in a sauce pan, and the pieces of turtle and cook a little; pour in some broth; put in your dish a lemon cut in slices, an egg boiled and cut up; pour over it the soup and meat and serve.   PROF. BLOT.

BLACK, OR TURTLE BEAN SOUP.

Take two teacups of beans, and soak them in water over night; then add three quarts of stock; let it boil three hours; adding mace, cinnamon, allspice and pepper, according to taste; two onions; pass through the cullender, and then through the sieve; put in the tureen the juice of two lemons, four eggs boiled hard and chopped fine, a little Harvey sauce, then pour the soup on it.

MRS. CHAS. CULLIS, Boston.

TOMATO SOUP.

Twelve tomatoes, peeled and cooked, or one quart can; one tablespoonful soda; one quart milk; season with salt and pepper; just before taking up, put in half a pint of crackers or bread crumbs, piece of butter size of an egg.

SCALLOPED LOBSTER.

Butter a deep dish; cover the bottom and sides with fine crumbs of bread; put in a layer of chopped boiled lobster, with pepper and a little salt; cover with crumbs and a little butter; add another layer of lobster, pepper and salt; cover as before; put in the liquor of the lobster; bake about twenty minutes. A good substitute for oysters in warm weather.   MRS. JOSEPH STORY, Boston.

LOBSTER FARSEE.

Chop the Lobster fine; add a small lump of butter, half a cup of cream or milk, salt and pepper; make into small cakes; put a piece of butter on each cake; bake twenty minutes.

FISH PUDDING.

Take three pounds of fresh Cod or any other white fish; boil in the evening and after cooking take out the bones and mince quite fine; in the morning make a drawn butter sauce of one pint of milk, three eggs, a little flour, butter, salt and pepper; boil all together and mix with the fish; put all in a pudding dish and bake half an hour.

FISH SAUCE.

Beat a teacup of butter to a cream; add a little French and English mustard, the juice of one lemon and chopped cucumber pickle.

FRESH FISH WARMED OVER.

One pint of fish picked fine, one quart of milk, two eggs, one-fourth of a cup of flour, mixed with a little of the milk; pepper, salt and nutmeg, one-fourth of a teaspoonful each. Mix smoothly the milk, flour, eggs and spice. Set this sauce over the fire and stir until thick as cream. Put in a deep dish alternately, the sauce, fish and bread crumbs in the order mentioned; brown lightly in the oven.

MRS. KRUM.

Half a pound of veal, half a pound of suet chopped fine, a few sweet herbs and parsley cut fine, a little pounded mace and a small nutmeg, a little lemon peel grated, pepper and salt, the yolks of two eggs; mix all of them well together, then roll them into small round balls, roll them in flour and fry them brown. If they are for anything white, put a little water in a saucepan, and when the water boils put them in and let them boil for a few minutes.

Mrs. Sam'l Treat.

TO BOIL A LEG OF VEAL.

Put the meat in boiling water, with a few slices of pork in it. When done make a gravy of drawn butter. Time for cooking two to three hours.

VEAL CUTLET.

The nicest cutlets are from the round; about half an inch thick; season with salt and pepper; dip into beaten egg, then in flour. Put into a skillet with hot lard, and fry a nice brown. When done, take out, make a gravy with a little flour and water.

HAUNCH OF VENISON.

Take the venison, wash and dry well; butter a sheet of white paper, and cover it over the venison; then cover with two or three more thicknesses of strong paper, tied on with strong twine; put into the pan, and as soon as in the oven baste the paper well and constantly to keep from burning; about thirty minutes before being done, which can be told by running a skewer in, and if tender, 'tis done; remove the papers, and dredge the meat with flour and baste with butter, until a nice brown color. Must be served on very hot plates, and currant jelly passed around.

POTTED BEEF.

Take three pounds of lean beef, put it on to boil covered with water; let it simmer until perfectly tender, when it will be easily chopped: chop it in a wooden bowl; then pound it in a marble mortar or bowl, adding gradually the liquor in which the meat was boiled; some nice marrow from the beef bones should be added before the meat is done, but if you have no marrow add a little melted butter as you pound. Season it with pepper and salt to taste, with a little cloves, allspice and grated nutmeg may be added. When finely pounded put it in small jars, press it down, and the next day cover it with melted butter which will preserve it much longer than if left open. Veal may be done in the same way, omitting spices except mace.

BEEF A LA MODE.

Take a round of fresh beef and beat it well to make it tender. Rub it all over with salt and pepper, lard it on both sides with bacon; put a calf's foot, a few onions, a carrot cut in pieces, a bunch of sweet herbs cut small, one or two laurel leaves, some cloves and a beaten nutmeg in the pan. Pour in a half a pint of red wine and a half a pint of white wine, a spoonful of brandy. Let it stew slowly six hours; take it out and strain the gravy; pour it on the meat and serve. Venison is very nice done in the same way; both are better prepared the night before.

SPICED BEEF.

Purchase of your butcher a round of beef of twelve or sixteen pounds weight; let it lay in salt two hours; take it out; wash clean; rub with salt and saltpetre until very red; then take a tablespoonful each of allspice, mace and black pepper; mix them with the marrow which comes out of the bone; let it lay nine days in this mixture, turning and rubbing it every day; then tie it closely in a cloth and steam it by the following process. Put your vessel for cooking it over the fire with a quart of water; place some sticks in the vessel and lay your meat upon it; renew the water whenever it evaporates. Steam three hours or until you can put a fork through it. This dish is highly esteemed in the south for lunches. To be eaten cold.   MRS. WELLS.

HASH.

Take cold beef of any kind; chop fine; then take about one-third mashed potatoes; season with salt and pepper; very little water. It is also very nice to leave out the potatoes; have some slices of bread toasted, laid on the platter, and pour the meat on the toast.

MEAT PIE.

Cut up meat in slices; season with salt, pepper, onion and parsley; cover with tomatoes and bread crumbs; butter on top.

TO WARM COLD MEATS.

Chop the meat fine; add salt, pepper, a little onion and tomato catsup; fill a baking dish one-third full, cover it over with boiled potatoes mashed with milk; lay bits of butter on top, and bake fifteen or twenty minutes.

MYSTERY.

Take any kind of cold meat chopped fine, with cold ham or salt pork; season with salt and pepper, and mix in two eggs and a little butter; mix this with rusk crumbs, and bake like pudding or put in a skillet and warm like hash, or put into balls, flatten and fry like sausages.

BEEF OMELET.

Two pounds raw beef chopped fine; one egg well beaten, two crackers pounded fine; piece of butter size of one-half an egg melted. Pepper, salt and sage to taste; mix well together with a little flour on kneading board. Bake one hour in pan with a little water; baste often; slice when cold.

RICHAMELLA.

Mince your cold roast veal in a chopping bowl; leave out the stringy part; put into the frying pan a teacupful or more of milk or sweet cream, into which stir, when hot, a tablespoonful of butter and flour, well mixed together; then add veal. Heat it well through; grate a little nutmeg or fine mace over. Delicious for breakfast; can be used for veal patties.   MRS. D. YOUNG.

VEAL FRICANDEAU.

Take a small fillet without a bone, lard it well with pork, putting it into the meat where there is no skin; butter the chafing-dish (some people lay a slice or two of bacon in the dish), put the meat in larded side up, place therein four carrots, four onions, a bunch of parsley, thyme or marjoram, two or three cloves, two glasses of water, and a little pepper. If the piece weigh three or four pounds, it must stew for three hours gently, covered close. Before serving take out the carrots and onions, baste the meat well with the gravy, take off all the fat, add to it a spoonful of brown flour and one glass of wine, stir it well in and pour it over the meat; to serve it add to the gravy either tomato ketchup, sorrel or spinach as you choose.

MRS. SAM'L TREAT.

VEAL OLIVES.

Slice as large pieces as you can get from a leg of veal; make a stuffing of grated bread, butter, a little onion minced, salt, pepper, and spread over the slices. Beat an egg and put over the stuffing. Roll each slice up tightly, and tie with a thread; stick a few cloves in them; grate bread thickly over them after being put in the skillet, with butter and onions chopped fine; when done lay them on a dish; make your gravy and pour over them; take the threads off, and garnish with eggs, boiled hard, and serve. To be cut in slices.   MRS. U. S. GRANT.

4

BAKED TOMATOES.

Fill a deep dish with whole tomatoes skinned; sprinkle with bread crumbs, one tablespoonful of sugar, same of butter, salt and pepper to taste. Tomatoes may be sliced and cooked in the same way.

STUFFED BAKED TOMATOES.

Bake the tomatoes whole; then scoop out a small hole at the top and fill with fried bread crumbs and onions, or bread crumbs with butter, sugar, salt and pepper; then brown the tomatoes in an oven, and take care that the skin does not break.

FRIED TOMATOES.

Wash them, cut in slices; make a batter of flour, water and egg, and season with pepper and salt; dip each piece in the batter; have ready some melted butter in a pan; put them in it, and fry slowly till nicely brown.

MISS E. L. GLOVER.

STEWED TOMATOES.

Slice the tomatoes into a lined saucepan; season them with pepper and salt, and place small pieces of butter on them; cover the lid down closely, and stew from twenty to twenty five minutes, or until the tomatoes are perfectly tender. Bread crumbs may be added if desired to thicken; a minced onion—a small one—improves the flavor. Another variety is, to add a quarter as much green corn as tomatoes, into the saucepan when first put on the fire.

BOILED GREEN CORN.

Take young sugar corn; clean by stripping off the outer leaves; turn back the innermost covering, pick off the silk and recover the ear with the husk that grew nearest it; tie at the top; put in boiling salted water, and cook fast about half an hour; send to the table wrapped in a napkin.

SUCCOTASH.

Cut from the cob, not too closely, young sugar corn; scraping off with a knife what is left on the cob. Take a third more corn than beans, when the former has been cut from the cob, and the latter shelled; put the beans into boiling water enough to cover them, and cook half an hour before the corn is put on, which should be boiled half an hour; put both together; add a cup of rich milk or cream, a large piece of butter, salt and pepper to taste; cook slowly for half an hour; watch closely to prevent burning.

MARY COLBURT.

SUCCOTASH.

One quart of Lima beans put on in two quarts of cold water; while boiling cut the corn from a dozen ears, and boil the cobs for a few minutes with the beans; when the beans are done, stir the corn with the beans, and add one cup of cream, one tablespoon of butter, one teaspoon of sugar, salt and pepper to taste; the corn should cook twenty minutes. A small piece of salt pork cooked with the beans is a great improvement. MRS. C. B. RICHARDS.

STEWED GREEN CORN.

Cut from the cob and stew in boiling water, fifteen minutes; turn off most of the water; cover with cold milk, and stew until tender, adding a large lump of butter, cut in small pieces, rolled in flour; season with salt and pepper to taste.

CORN CAKES OR MOCK OYSTERS.

One pint of grated green corn, three tablespoons of milk, one-half cup of melted butter, one teaspoon of salt, one-half of pepper, one egg; bake on a griddle; flour to stiffen.

LIMA BEANS.

Boil about an hour; pour the water off; season with salt, pepper and butter; send to the table hot.

Dried Lima beans must be soaked over night, and boiled two hours, or until they are soft, and should have some um added to the dressing.

BREAD AND BUTTER PUDDING.

Cut some slices of bread moderately thick, without the crust, butter, and cover the bottom of a buttered dish with them; spread a pound of currants, raisins, or stewed apples over the slices, strew some brown sugar over it; put another layer of bread and fruit, etc., with a layer of bread for the top, then pour over the whole four eggs, mixed with a pint of milk; bake one hour; grate nutmeg over it when done; serve warm.

PUDDING FRUIT.

Take apple sauce or stewed pears, or peaches, or any kind of small berries, and mix them with equal quantities of rusk crumbs; make a custard of four eggs, one quart of milk, sweetening very sweet; mix it with the crumbs and bake twenty minutes.   MRS. D. YOUNG.

BREAD MERINGUE.

Rub stale bread (for a small family about a pint); add milk to make a little thicker than custard, lump of butter the size of an egg, yolks of four eggs, sweetened; let it bake until a light brown; take it out and cover up with jelly, any kind you like; beat the whites of eggs, flavor and sweeten, spread over the top; bake a few minutes; eat cold. Some serve with cream.   MRS. BROCK.

BAKED INDIAN PUDDING.

Boil one quart of milk and one pint of fine Indian meal, stirring it well; mix three tablespoonfuls of flour with one pint of milk until free from lumps; mix this with the Indian meal and stir the mixture well. When moderately warm, stir in three beaten eggs, two spoonfuls of sugar, one tea-spoonful of salt, two of cinnamon or nutmeg, and one table-spoonful of melted butter. When baked five or six minutes stir in raisins and one-half pint of milk.

                              MRS. S. R. FILLEY.

8

ITALIAN SNOW.

Half a box of Cox's gelatine to one pint of cold water, whites of three eggs, one cup of sugar, flavoring of any kind of extract, beat with egg-beater for twenty minutes, pour into moulds, thoroughly dissolve the gelatine before adding the eggs. To be eaten with cream.

MRS. E. J. CLARK, Carondelet.

APPLE SNOW.

Put twelve tart apples in cold water and set them over a slow fire; when soft drain off the water, strip off the skins, core, and lay them in a deep dish; beat the whites of twelve eggs to a froth, put in half a pound of powdered sugar to the apples, beat to a stiff froth, and add the beaten eggs; beat the whole to a stiff snow, turn into a dessert dish, and ornament with myrtle or box.

APPLE FLOAT.

Sweeten and season with mace or nutmeg, a small bowl of apple sauce (which has been through a sieve); then add the whites of three eggs beaten to a stiff froth. Eat with cream and sugar.   MRS. R. H. MORTON.

ORANGE SOUFFLE.

Peel and slice three oranges, one pint of milk, yolks of five eggs; sweeten to taste. When done pour on oranges; beat the whites to a froth; pour gently over oranges; put in oven and brown.   MRS. SARAH DAVIS.

OMELET SOUFFLE.

One cup of flour, one pint of milk, one spoonful of sugar, butter size of a walnut, scald milk, flour and butter together; after the batter is cold stir in the yolks of five eggs; stir in the whites of the eggs well beaten just before baking. Bake in a quick oven; eat with sauce. This is a splendid pudding.   MISS E. H. GLOVER.

BREAD PUDDING.

One quart of milk, one pint of bread crumbs, half a cup of butter, four eggs, one cup of sugar; heat milk and butter; add the yolks of eggs and sugar beaten, with a little cold milk, thin the bread, put in the oven, and add the whites of the eggs, well beaten, just before taking out.

Updated Version

Ingredients:

1 cup milk
4 eggs
4 egg whites
½ cup sugar
1 tablespoon vanilla extract
½ teaspoon cinnamon
4 cups whole grain bread, cut into cubes
2 cups frozen cherries, thawed
¾ semisweet chocolate chips
½ cup sliced almonds, divided in half

Directions:

Preheat oven to 375 degrees. Whisk milk, egg, and egg whites in a bowl, then add in sugar, vanilla, and cinnamon. In a separate bowl, mix the cherries, chocolate chips, and half of the almonds. Pour the egg mixture on top and then stir until combined. Transfer to a greased 2 quart casserole or 9 x 13 baking dish, cover with foil, and bake for 40 minutes. Take the remaining almonds and lightly toast on the stovetop in a dry pan. After the bread pudding has baked for 40 minutes, remove the foil and sprinkle the toasted almonds on top. Bake for another 20 minutes, uncovered, then remove from oven to cool.

Fish, Flesh and Fowl—
A Cook Book
(1894)

Fish, Flesh and Fowl—A Cook Book was published by the Ladies of State Street Parish, Portland, Maine, in 1894. The Cathedral Church of St. Luke, pictured below, is located at 143 State St.

FISH, FLESH AND FOWL

A COOK BOOK

— OF —

*Valuable Recipes, all of which have been thoroughly
and successfully tested*

COMPILED BY

LADIES OF STATE STREET PARISH

PORTLAND

TRANSCRIPT PRINTING HOUSE, 44 EXCHANGE STREET

1894

"The Lord sends meat; the Devil cooks,"
 Of old a proverb was,
What slander on the gentle sex!
 What charge without a cause!

The Woman Question is, no doubt,
 "Where doth my mission lie?
Shall all our aspirations tend
 To pudding, cake and pie?"

Could man be made to comprehend
 The aggravation sore,
Of frosting, roasting, broiling—all
 The varied kitchen lore—

'Twould all come right then, bye and bye,
 Disproved all slanders rife;
We'd get with jubilation,
 Our *Desserts* in this life.

SOUPS.

"Now good digestion wait on appetite."
—[SHAKESPEARE.

Stock. Take lean beef and cold water, in proportion of one pound of beef to one quart water; place it in a soup kettle over a good fire; when it boils add cup of cold water and remove the scum; then place the kettle over a moderate fire and let it simmer slowly four or five hours; this stock may be used for all soups in which meat broth is desired.

Black Bean. One pint black beans, soaked over night; in the morning pour off the water, add a gallon of water, with any bones, either of beef or mutton, (very little meat needed), and boil several hours; season with salt and pepper; take off all the fat, strain the soup and let it boil again before serving; cut a lemon in thin slices and put into the tureen and pour the soup upon it; some add cloves and yolks of hard boiled eggs.

Beef. Take sufficient soup stock; boil one onion, one carrot, one quart potatoes, and vegetables to suit taste, in a little water, and strain into the soup stock; add pepper, salt, etc., to suit.

Bouillon. Put a shank of beef (six or seven pounds) into a large pot and cover with cold water; leave on front of stove until it boils, then move it to the back of stove and let it simmer an hour and a half; cut up two carrots, two onions, and half a lemon; salt to taste, and boil until the meat falls from the bones; then strain through a sieve and set in the cold; next day remove every particle of grease that has risen to the top; heat the bouillon and pour into cups, first having a slice of lemon in each cup; season to taste.

Celery. Five heads of celery, one pint good soup stock, three of water, one-half pint cream or rich milk; cut the celery into inch lengths, put on with the water and cook until tender; take out the celery and rub through a sieve ; add to the soup stock and cook slowly one-half hour; heat the cream and stir into it one tablespoon flour rubbed into one tablespoon butter, cook five minutes; pour into the celery, heat very hot but not boil, and serve.

Corn. One quart milk, one pint green corn (cut from the cob), two eggs, butter, pepper and salt to suit the taste. Cook half an hour.

Lobster. Three crackers pounded fine, mixed with the tomally, piece butter size of an egg; boil one quart milk, and pour on the paste, stirring all the time until smooth; chop the lobster fine, put into the mixture, and boil, not too long, as it will make it tough. Pepper and salt.

Mock Oyster. Six ripe tomatoes skinned and boiled in a pint of water, and a teaspoon saleratus, then add a quart of sweet milk, and four crackers pounded. Season with pepper and salt.

Noodle. Two eggs, thicken with enough flour to roll out very thin, let dry two hours, roll and cut very thin; boil twenty minutes in chicken already prepared for soup. Season with onions.

FISH.

"With hooks and nets you catch us,
   You never regard our pains;
Yet we reward you with dainty food,
   To strengthen your body and brains."

Baked Cod. Pour boiling water over the fish, and keep hot an hour; then take it off the bone and put in a dish with a quart of milk, half an onion, one-quarter pound butter, very little thickening of flour, little salt, and cover with bread crumbs. Bake an hour and a half.

Baked Fish. Take a fish weighing from four to six pounds, wash clean, season with salt; make a dressing with five crackers rolled fine, one tablespoon butter, one teaspoon salt, little pepper, one-half teaspoon chopped parsley, water enough to make moist, stuff the fish with this preparation, fasten with skewer, cut slits in fish, put in strips of salt pork, dredge with flour. Bake one hour, basting often. Serve with tomato sauce.

Baked Lobster. Two or three lobsters chopped fine, season with pepper, salt and a tablespoon melted butter, one pint milk thickened with a tablespoon of flour, one teaspoon of mustard. Mix all together and bake with cracker crumbs on top.

Baked Shad Roe. Wash and cook three shad roes in boiling water, salted, with one tablespoon vinegar for ten minutes. Place on a buttered plate, cover with tomato sauce and bake thirty minutes, basting twice.

MEATS.

"God sendeth and giveth both mouth and the meat."

How to Choose Meats. It is always important to know how to choose meat in buying. Ox beef should be of fine grain or fibre, the flesh or lean of a bright red color and firm, the fat white, and distributed throughout the lean; it should not be yellow or semi-fluid. If the meat is entirely lean, it will be tough and its nutritive power is low. Veal is dry if fresh. It should be close-grained. If the meat is moist and flabby it is stale. Mutton should be of a clear, deep pink tint; firm, and with a liberal supply of fat. Fine wether mutton may be recognized by the presence of a small mass of fat on the upper part of the leg. It is more nutricious than ordinary mutton, the darker its tint the finer its flavor. Pork should be of a pale deep pink tint, and the fat very firm. If it is soft or the fat is yellow the meat is bad. If it is semi-fluid the animal has probably been fed on flesh.

Potted Beef. Take a large beef shank and put it into cold water to cover it, boil until perfectly tender, remove bone and cartilage, chop the meat fine and replace it in the kettle with the liquor which should be one quart, let it simmer gently and season with salt, pepper and mace to suit the taste. Press and cut in slices for lunch or tea.

Croquettes. To use up small, nice pieces of meat, chop them fine, and mix bread crumbs, a little broth or gravy, an egg, pepper and salt. Make into cakes and roll in flour, and fry in hot drippings.

Meat Pie. Cut up some good, tender, raw beef or mutton, season with pepper, salt, and if liked one finely chopped onion; boil half dozen good sized potatoes, when done, mash smooth and wet with milk enough to make a dough to make the crust, salt to taste; roll out full half an inch thick, and line a buttered dish large enough to hold the meat; lay in the meat, add a teacup of water or a little less, then roll out a thick crust of the potato, covering the top of the pie at least an inch thick, and bake about an hour and a half.

Meat and Potato Pie. Butter a baking dish; put in layer of cold mashed potatoes, or sliced ones, but if these are used, small pieces of butter must be added; on the potato put a layer of meat cut in small pieces, little salt, pepper and a few rings of onions; then more potato, and in this way fill the dish having the top potato. Before the last layer of potato, pour in any gravy you may have; bake until the potato is a nice brown.

Devilled Ham. One pint boiled ham chopped fine with a good proportion of fat, one teaspoon dry mustard, one tablespoon flour, one-half cup boiling water. Press in a mould and cut in slices.

Roast Lamb and Mint Sauce. Stuff a hind quarter of lamb with fine bread crumbs, pepper, salt and butter; rub the outside with salt, pepper, butter and flour; then roast two hours. Mint sauce:—Chop the mint fine; pour on a little hot water; let it stand on the stove a short time, then add a little vinegar and sugar to taste.

Sausages. Six pounds lean and two pounds fat pork, four tablespoons salt, six of sage, four of pepper, two of cloves.

To Chop Suet. Sprinkle flour over it while chopping, which will prevent the pieces from adhering.

Veal Loaf. 1. Three pounds raw veal, one-quarter pound salt pork (less will do if a little butter is used), chop fine, mix with two eggs, one cup cracker crumbs, three teaspoons salt, two of pepper, one tablespoon sage; press hard into a pudding dish and bake two hours. To be sliced when cold.

2. Three and a half pounds of raw veal, three slices salt pork chopped fine, six crackers pounded fine, two eggs beaten, tablespoon salt, teaspoon pepper, two pinches allspice, one of cloves, knead all together into a loaf, egg it over, put bits of butter on the top and scatter pounded cracker. Bake two hours basting with water.

Minced Veal. Three and one-half pounds of veal chopped fine, four eggs well beaten, four crackers pounded fine, one tablespoon salt, the same of pepper, one-half tablespoon nutmeg, three tablespoons cream or milk, butter the size of an egg. Mix all together in a loaf and bake two hours.

Veal Cutlets. Cut veal into pieces for serving; season with salt and pepper; dredge with flour (or egg and crumbs); brown in salt pork fat; put into stew pan; make brown gravy; season highly with vegetables cut fine or Worcestershire sauce. Pour over meat and simmer till tender (one and one-half hours).

Timbales. Mince and season meat with salt and pepper; add one egg and about one-half as much bread crumbs as meat; make moist enough with gravy and put in thoroughly buttered cups and bake in pan of water or not.

Camelons. Made same as Timbales, but baked in a roll one-half hour and served with tomato sauce around it.

FOWL.

"And as an ev'ning dragon came,
Assailant on the perched roosts
And nests in order rang'd
Of tame villatic fowl."

—[MILTON.

Chicken Pie. Cut into pieces the chickens, boil in enough water to cover until tender, adding when half done one tablespoon salt; take out chicken, keep warm, and thicken the liquid with one tablespoon each flour and butter rubbed together; add salt and pepper to taste; boil five minutes; take one quart flour, two teaspoons Cleveland's baking powder, little salt and one small cup butter; mix as biscuit. Take half, roll one-quarter inch thick and line a deep dish, leaving an inch over the sides to turn up over top crust; put in chicken, pour over gravy, cover with the other crust, with a large hole in center for steam to escape. Wet the edge and fold over the under crust, press firmly together; spread soft butter over the top, make ornament to fit the center and bake until done.

Chicken in Jelly. Boil a chicken or chickens in as little water as possible until the meat falls from the bones; pick off the meat, cut it rather fine, and season well with pepper and salt; put into the bottom and sides of a mould slices of hard-boiled eggs and fill nearly full with chicken. Boil down the broth till there is about a cupful left; season it well and pour over the chicken. It will form a jelly around the chicken. Let it stand on the ice over night or all day. To be sliced at table; garnish with fringed celery. If there is fear of the jelly not being stiff enough a little gelatine may be soaked and added.

Chicken Croquettes. One pound cooked chicken chopped fine, one-fourth pound white bread, one-fourth pound butter, four eggs, three large teaspoons finely chopped parsley, pinch of mace and nutmeg, one teaspoon salt, one pinch cayenne pepper; pour enough boiling water over the bread to soften it, place on the fire with the yolks of two eggs and cook until smooth; set away to cool, while mixing the chicken with the rest of the eggs unbeaten, two tablespoons thick cream, the butter and seasoning; beat all thoroughly together till nicely mixed; let the mixture get quite cold before forming into croquettes. A famous Southern receipt.

Maryland Chicken. Singe, remove fine feathers, cut into pieces for serving, wipe, season with salt and pepper, dip in egg, roll in fine cracker crumbs; put pieces into a buttered dish and bake one hour, basting very often with one-third cup butter and one cup water. Serve with cream sauce.

Pressed Chicken. Boil chicken very tender; be sure to have plenty of liquor; separate white meat from the dark; soak three slices of bread in the liquor for a few minutes, then chop it up with the dark meat. Put white meat in the bottom of the dish, pour a little liquor on, then put on a layer of dark meat, leave until it is cold, and it will turn out like jelly.

Roast Duck. After the duck is drawn, wipe the inside with a clean cloth and prepare dressing as follows: One cup pounded cracker, moisten with hot milk or water, three medium sized onions, parboil and chop fine, little butter, sage, pepper and salt to taste; mix all together and fill the crop and body of the duck, leaving room for the dressing to swell; reserve the liver, gizzard and heart for gravy; tie the body of the duck firmly with a string (which is buttered to keep from burning), and put in the oven. Baste first with salt and water, and then with its own gravy, dredging them last with a little flour.

Potted Pigeons. Make dressing the same as for turkey, stuff them and fry in pork fat until nicely browned; take them out, pour the fat into a kettle with little water, put them into this, and let them simmer half an hour or more. When done, take them out, thicken the broth a little and pour over them.

Turkey. For a ten pound turkey take two pints bread crumbs, half teacup butter, cut in small pieces, one teaspoon summer savory, pepper and salt; fill turkey with little of the dressing, few strained oysters, alternating until filled. Put the oyster liquid in the pan with a pint of water; bake in a moderate oven.

PUDDINGS.

"The daintiest last, to make the end more sweet."
[—KING RICHARD II.

Apple. One quart flour, one pint milk, one teaspoon soda, two teaspoons cream tartar, and small piece butter; roll out and fill with sliced apples; steam three hours. Served with sauce.

Apple Charlotte. Butter an earthen dish, and place around the sides slices of bread which have been cut about one inch thick, then soak in cold water and spread with butter, fill dish with sliced apple, grate over them one nutmeg, add one cup sugar, one cup water; cover with slices of bread which have been soaked and buttered and place a large plate over the dish and bake four hours; remove from the oven and let it get cool. When ready to serve, loosen around the edges with a knife and turn out on a dish. Serve with sugar and cream.

Apple Cream. Three tart apples, baked slowly (be careful not to brown the pulp); remove the skin and cores and strain, add one and one-half cups sugar, whites of two eggs, beaten stiff, and juice of one lemon; beat to a stiff froth. Serve with boiled custard made of the yolks of the eggs.

Charlotte Russe. One-third box gelatine dissolved in a coffee cup milk, one pint cream, sweetened and flavored with vanilla; beat together and let it stand until it begins to stiffen, then stir in the beaten whites of five eggs; line a dish with thin slices of plain cake (sponge being best), and pour in the mixture and set away to harden. When ready to serve, turn out on a dish.

Chocolate. Boil two cups bread crumbs in one quart milk till it thickens then let it cool; beat the yolks of five and the whites of two eggs with one cup sugar and three tablespoons grated chocolate, and add to the cooled mixture and bake one-half hour; beat the whites of three eggs with five tablespoons sugar and a small teaspoon vanilla, and spread over the pudding when cold and brown lightly. Eat cold with or without cream.

College. Yolks of two eggs, one-half cup sugar, one-half cup butter, one cup milk, one pint flour, teaspoon cream tartar, one-half teaspoon soda. SAUCE: Whites of two eggs, one and one-half cups sugar and juice of one lemon beaten stiff.

Cottage. One cup sugar, one egg, three tablespoons melted butter, one cup milk, two cups flour, one teaspoon cream tartar, one-half teaspoon soda. Bake one-half hour. Serve with hot sauce.

Cracker. One quart milk, eight tablespoons pounded cracker, four tablespoons sugar, five eggs, one-half pound raisins, piece of butter on top. Bake one-half hour.

Columbia. Two and one-half cups flour, one cup molasses, one cup sour milk, one-half teaspoon cinnamon, one teaspoon soda, one-half cup chopped pork or suet, one-half cup raisins. Steam three hours.

DISHES FOR INVALIDS.

Beef Tea. Fill glass can with lean beef cut in small pieces; cover closely and set in kettle of cold water, let this come to a boil, and boil till the juice is all extracted.

Infant's Beef Tea. Three ounces each beef and veal; boil six hours in water having a quart when it is done, add salt and skim when cold. Take equal parts of milk, water and broth, boil a minute and sweeten if desired.

Chicken Tea. Remove skin and fat from a chicken, cut in small pieces; boil in one quart water, with a little salt, for twenty minutes. Pour off the tea before the meat is quite cold.

Baked Milk. Bake two quarts milk eight or ten hours in a moderate oven in a jar covered with writing paper tied down. It will be thick like cream. Good for weak persons.

Eau Sucre. Dissolve three or four lumps loaf sugar in a glass of ice water, and take teaspoon every four minutes for a " tickling in the throat," or hacking cough.

Lemon Moss. Put a few sprigs of moss, which has been well washed, to soak in water enough to make the drink the thickness of cream. After standing a short time, add lemon juice and loaf sugar.

Toast Water. Slices of toast, nicely browned, without a symptom of burning; enough boiling water to cover them; cover closely and let them steep till cold; strain the water, sweeten to taste, and cool with ice. A bit of lemon juice can be added.

Meat Pie
See page 110 for original recipe.

Updated Version

Ingredients:
2 1/2 pounds of potatoes, peeled
1 tablespoon olive oil
2 onions, diced
4 cloves of garlic, minced
2 pounds ground beef
4 large carrots, peeled and chopped
3 ribs of celery, chopped
1 cup of frozen peas, thawed
1 cup dry red wine
3 tablespoons of flour (or more, if needed)
½ teaspoon dried marjoram
½ teaspoon thyme
½ to ¾ cup milk
2 tablespoons butter
Salt and pepper
½ cup Parmesan cheese
1 egg, lightly beaten

Directions:
Preheat oven to 425 degrees. Boil the potatoes in water until they are tender, about 10 minutes.

While potatoes are cooking, heat the oil in a large skillet. Add garlic and onion and sautée for about 2 minutes. Add ground beef, carrots, and celery, cook until beef is browned. Pour the wine into the skillet, along with the herbs and thawed peas. Stir in the flour by the tablespoon until the pan juices have a thick consistency, like gravy. Remove from heat and put the ground beef mixture in a greased 9 x 13 casserole dish.

When potatoes are tender, drain the water off and mash them. Add butter and milk until they are smooth. Season with salt and pepper, mix in the Parmesan cheese, and add the egg. Gently spread the potatoes on top of the meat in the casserole dish and bake for 30 minutes, or until browned on top.

Hawaiian Cook Book

(1920)

The sixth edition of the *Hawaiian Cook Book* was compiled by the Womans' Society of the Central Union Church of Honolulu, Hawaii, and published in 1920. Its aim was to feature Hawaiian food products, especially fish, cooked by "Hawaiian methods."

Central Union traces its roots to the whaling ships that began visiting Hawaii in 1819. The present church is commonly referred to as the "Church in a Garden," as its worship, education, and administrative buildings are set in landscaped grounds characterized by large lawns and mature trees, including monkeypod, kiawe, plumeria, Norfolk Island pine, royal palm, and coconut palm trees. The Sanctuary, built in 1924, was placed on the State Register of Historic Places in 2006.

Kedegeree (A Breakfast or Lunch Dish)

2 c. boiled or steamed fish flaked

2 c. boiled rice

2 hard-boiled eggs

2 T. butter substitute

Seasoning

Chopped parsley

Put rice and fish into a double boiler with the butter substitute, seasoning and parsley. Stir lightly with a fork without mashing. When hot all through, pile on a hot dish; cut eggs into 8 parts and stand around edges. A few rolls of crisp bacon are good with this; if used, the bacon fat may replace the butter substitute.

Fish Pie

Cold fish

Seasoning

Hot mashed potatoes

Butter substitute

Remove the bones and skin from any cold cooked fish, shred it, and add seasoning to taste. Grease a baking dish, cover the bottom with potatoes, and add the fish and small bits of butter substitute. Season, cover with a top layer of potatoes, and bake in a hot oven 10 minutes, or until brown.

Fish Pudding

2½ or 3 c. scraped raw fish

¾ c. cream

¼ c. bread crumbs

4 eggs

Mix bread crumbs, cream and yolks of eggs with the fish; then add beaten whites, salt and pepper. Place in steamer, top having central opening as in angel cake tin, cover, and steam uninterruptedly for 25 minutes. Serve with cream sauce.

Fish Pudding

Awa, Awa-aua, or Oio

1 tin mushrooms

½ c. bread crumbs

4 eggs

¾ c. cream

Seasoning

Grate raw fish, mash to pulp, and season to taste; add bread crumbs, the mushrooms (chopped), the unbeaten yolks of eggs, and the cream (whipped). Just before placing in the steamer, which should be greased, add well-beaten whites of eggs. Steam 25 minutes, and serve immediately with cream sauce and mushrooms. A delicious way to use these fish, which are too bony to be cooked by other methods.

Salmon Pudding

1 lb. salmon	½ t. mustard
2 eggs	Salt and pepper
1 c. milk	Cayenne
1 T. flour	Onion
1 T. butter substitute	Celery
1 T. gelatine	Green pepper
1 t. sugar	

Boil the salmon, remove skin and bones, shred fine, and mix with chopped hard-boiled egg, onion, celery, and green pepper. Then prepare a cream by heating milk, with flour, butter substitute, sugar, mustard, salt and pepper, until it comes to a boil; then add 1 beaten egg and cayenne pepper. When cream is cool, add gelatine, soaked, and dissolve in hot water, and pour over fish. Put in mould, and place on ice.

Fish in Ramekins

1½ lbs. fish	1 c. hot milk
Bread crumbs	Curry powder
2 T. butter substitute	Salt
1 T. flour	

Boil and flake fish. Make a white sauce with the butter substitute, flour, and milk; season with salt and a little curry powder; and mix lightly with fish. Fill the dishes, cover with butter and seasoned bread crumbs, and brown in the oven. Garnish with parsley.

Rechauffe of Fish

2 c. cold boiled fish	1 egg
2 T. butter substitute	1 c. cracker or bread crumbs
½ c. milk or cream	Seasoning

Cut fish in small pieces, and put in chafing dish with butter substitute, milk, crumbs, salt and pepper, and egg slightly beaten. Simmer for five or six minutes.

___

Salad (Good for Picnics)

Have cold boiled or steamed fish flaked with no bones or skin. To every cup, add 1 c. boiled rice, half c. chopped celery, a little chopped parsley. Add enough mayonnaise to moisten and mould it. Season carefully. If anchovies are liked, cut in thin strips and decorate the salad with them. Served at a picnic, hard-boiled egg chopped fine is the best garnish.

___

Scalloped Fish

Cold fish	Chopped parsley
Cream sauce	Paprika
Bread crumbs	Seasoning

Place in baking dish alternate layers of bread crumbs, and minced fish and parsley, and pour on generously a rich cream sauce. Let top layer be of bread crumbs dotted with butter. Bake until well browned.

___

Fish Souffle

2 c. shredded fish	2 eggs (whites)
½ c. bread crumbs	1 T. butter substitute
1 c. milk	Seasoning

Mix bread crumbs, milk, butter substitute and seasoning; cook 5 minutes. Add fish and the whites of the eggs well beaten. Bake in cassscrole set in water from 20 to 30 minutes.

___

Fish Souffle

1 c. cold boiled fish	1 c. cream sauce
2 c. mashed or riced potatoes	1 t. salt
3 eggs	½ T. Worchestershire sauce or
Kitchen Bouquet	

Add the picked fish, cream sauce, and egg yolks well beaten

to the potatoes. Fold in lightly the whites of the eggs beaten till stiff. Brush a baking pan with a little cooking oil, put in the mixture, rough it on top, and bake till light-brown. Serve at once.

SPECIALS

Aawa

After the fish is carefully washed, put in the stuffing, and sew up the opening. Dredge the fish with salt, pepper, and flour, and lay it on slices of larding pork in a baking pan. Place slices of pork also over the back. Allow 15 minutes to each pound and baste frequently. The pork should supply sufficient liquid for basting; if not, add very little water.

Serve with brown sauce; garnish with lemon and parsley or watercress.

Aku (Portuguese Style)

Dice the fish, and cover with **vinegar.** Add a large onion (sliced), 2 pieces garlic (mashed), salt, and let stand 6 hours. Then fry in hot fat.

Akule

Clean, remove heads, and sprinkle with salt. Cut up 6 or 8 green onions and 3 large tomatoes (canned are equally good). Place fish in well-greased pan, cover over with onions and to-matoes, put cover on pan, and cook slowly 20 minutes or until done.

Mullet (Spanish Style)

Clean 2 or 3 mullet, cut into 3-inch pieces, and place in a kettle containing 1 T. Crisco. Add cut-up green onions, tomatoes, salt, and enough cooked rice to serve the family. Cook 30 minutes.

Mullet (Hawaiian Style)

Clean, sprinkle with salt, place on from 6 to 8 ti leaves,

bind with wire, and bake from 20 to 30 minutes.   Added cocoanut milk gives it a flavor.

_____

Boiled Mullet

Put mullet in saucepan, almost cover with water, add 1 T.
of salt, cook ½ hour.   Good served with poi.

Kala, Moi, Papiopio, and Akule are good this way.   The
Kala should be skinned before cooking.

_____

Boiled Mullet with Coconut Sauce

Boil mullet as above.   When nearly cooked throw half the
water away and in its place add juice of two cocoanuts.   To
secure this, grate cocoanuts, and extract juice by squeezing
through potato press.

_____

Boiled Mullet with White Sauce

Put mullet in saucepan, almost cover with water, and add
salt.   When done, lift carefully to a platter and pour over a
sauce made of 1 C. of milk, 1 T. flour, 1 T. butter substitute,
and 2 hard-boiled eggs, chopped up rather fine.   Moi and
Kumu are good cooked this way.

_____

Mullet in Ti Leaves

Procure 8 or 10 ti leaves.   Put salt on 2 or 3 medium-
sized fish, wrap in ti leaves, put in oven, and bake for ¾
hour.   Moi, Weke and Kumu are good this way.

_____

Fish With Cocoanut

Clean and prepare Mullet or Moi for baking in ti-leaves.
Salt them, pour into the stomach and gills cocoanut juice
secured by grating and squeezing the pulp of a cocoanut; tie
up in the ti-leaves and bake in the oven or broil on the coals
outdoors.   The latter method is preferable, for the juices do
not dry away so much as in an oven, and the leaves do not
stick to the fish, as they often do in the former case.

TO PREPARE COCOANUT JUICE FOR GRAVIES.

Grate the cocoanut and add a very little fresh milk, and let it stand on the back of the stove for half an hour, then turn it into a clean cloth and wring the juice very dry.

MOCK DUCK.—Mrs. John Wilder.

Take a steak, a large one is best, though if you can tie them up, pieces will do, even if small. Take out the large bone, and pound the beef; make a dressing of bread that has been soaked in water and squeezed as dry as possible, 2 pieces of bacon fried and chopped fine, with 1 large onion, or a number of small ones, sage, summer savory, a little butter, and plenty of salt and pepper. Make early in the morning—it is better, for standing. Cook it a little, stirring it all the time. Put the dressing in the steak, leaving out a little for the gravy. Tie it up tightly, beat an egg well, pour it all over the steak, put on 2 tablespoonfuls of butter in lumps, put it in a pan with water, but do not let the water touch it. Baste often. Cook about an hour.

Gravy for above.

Any cold meat gravy is nice with a little of the dressing, more onion, sage, savory, and a little bacon or cold beef minced very fine, and seasoned highly with salt and pepper.

BEEFSTEAK PIE.—Mrs. C. D. Miller.

Take about 2 pounds of steak, slice in pieces about seven inches long and 1/4 inch thick; dredge each piece with flour, pepper and salt sparingly, add a pinch of celery salt, shred two medium sized onions and sprinkle each piece. Ball these strips firmly (some tie them as in beef olives), put them in a saucepan, cover with boiling water and place on the stove where it will simmer (not boil fiercely) for one hour. Place in the middle of a deep pie dish an inverted tea-cup and lay the beef rolls around it. Prepare this in the morning then set it in the safe. Strain the liquor and set it aside to cool, then remove the fat and heat the liquor; when near the boiling point stir in one dessert spoonful of butter rubbed with two of flour (rub it very smooth), add to the liquor and stir till it is smooth and creamy, then pour this over the beef in the pie dish and cover with the crust, making two incisions to allow the steam to escape. Chicken cut up and prepared in the same way is delicious. Use any good pie crust being sure to cut incision on top.

RUTH PINCH'S BEEFSTEAK PUDDING.—Mrs. Kinney.

Make into a firm smooth paste, 1 pound flour, 1 cup of suet chopped fine, a little salt with a little water. Line with this a basin which holds 1½ pints. Season and cut up a pound of tender steak, free from bone and skin, with an ounce of salt and ½ teaspoonful of pepper. Lay it in the crust, pour in ¼ pint of

HAMBURG CAKES.—Mrs. W. D. Alexander.

Chop a pound of round steak, add a grated minced onion, 1 egg, 1 cup rolled crackers and seasoning. Make into balls and drop into a hot pan without grease. This keeps in the juice and prevents the meat from being greasy.

———

BEEFSTEAK ROLLS.—Mrs. Kittredge.

Cut thin slices of round steak, a little larger than a slice of baker's roll, as many slices of bread as of the steak. Butter the bread, stick in a few cloves and sprinkle with pepper and celery salt. Roll the slice of steak over into the bread with a firm roll and tie up well with a string. Dredge each roll with flour. Put in a saucepan a tablespoon of butter, and fry the rolls till quite brown in the butter. Then remove them to a stewpan and add enough water to cover them. Let them simmer slowly for a couple of hours. Serve with the gravy. These are nice the next day, cold, cut in slices, without the gravy.

———

SPANISH FRICEO.—Miss Amelia Hoffman.

This dish is made from good beef (the same kind as is used for beefsteaks), lean pork or young mutton. The best is beef and pork in equal quantities. Two pounds of meat is enough for six or eight persons. The meat is beaten till soft and then cut in thin slices. Cut raw potatoes in thin slices, washing them before they are cut, but not after, and take 2 soup plates of them. Mix with the potatoes 2 saucersful of onions cut in slices. Take a pudding dish and put meat and potatoes in layers. Scatter over each layer some pepper and some Jamaica pepper and salt; put on every layer of potatoes a pieces of butter, and ¾ tablespoonful of thick sour cream. Close the pudding dish well and put it in boiling water, and let it boil for 1½ hours.

BREAD CROQUETTES.—Mrs. W. D. Alexander.

Chop the bread very fine, removing any hard or brown crust, soak with hot water, not too soft. To a pint bowlful of the bread allow a heaping teaspoonful of butter, 1 egg well beaten, salt, pepper, sifted sage to season well. Make into little cakes, dust in flour and fry a light brown. They are good without the egg, adding a rolled cracker with the seasoning.

GREEN CORN PUDDING—Mrs. W. W. Hall.

Four ears of corn, two eggs, 1 pint of milk, butter size of an egg, three tablespoonfuls of flour, salt and pepper. Cut the lines of corn down with a sharp knife, then with the back of the blade scrape from the cob; this leaves the hull of the corn on the cob, taking only the inner part. Beat the corn pulp thoroughly with the other ingredients; pour into a baking dish and bake one hour. Serve as a vegetable.

This same mixture stewed is very good.

VEGETABLE SUCCOTASH

5c. soup vegetables	1 cup raw rice
2 cups of water	Seasoning.
2 tablespoons butter	1 cube sugar.

Wash and cut up the vegetables in small dice. Put butter in saucepan, add the vegetables and cook without browning for ten minutes. Add the rice well washed, the seasoning and sugar, and the water boiling. Stir well, cover closely, and turn fire low. Cook for thirty-five minutes.

BREAD FRUIT.

Pick the breadfruit when yellow. Stand in a cold place, with salt around the stem. Leave until it is a little withered looking and the skin brown. Remove stalk and bake one hour in moderate oven. Split open by hand remove core, and serve with butter, pepper and salt as a vegetable.

BAKED BANANAS.

(Use plantain or cooking bananas.)

Baked whole in the skins, remove the ends and bake twenty minutes. Serve in the skins like a potato.

Second Receipe.—Peel, slice in half lengths, place on buttered dish and lemon juice squeezed over them, and bake twenty minutes.

Third Receipe.—Slice, sprinkle with lemon juice and sugar and put in buttered baking dish with first a layer of crumbs, then a layer of bananas with a layer of crumbs on top, dot with butter and bake till brown. Serve with curried dishes.

SALADS.

(Use sweet bananas). Sweet bananas cut in halves lengthwise, balls of cream cheese or cottage cheese sprinkled with chopped nuts between, the bananas dotted with mayonnaise.

Second receipe—Cut bananas in dice with equal quantities of chopped celery and a few chopped walnuts. Mix with mayonnaise and serve in half skins or on lettuce leaf.

Third Recipe—Cooking banana baked, cooled, skin removed and placed on lettuce leaf with mayonnaise and chopped nuts on top.

BANANA DUMPLINGS.

Slice and cut in pieces with sugar and cinnamon, cover with pastry as for apple dumpling and bake twenty minutes. Serve hot with cream.

BANANA CUSTARD.

Make a boiled custard and while hot pour over sliced bananas and let cool. A favorite with children.

BANANA BROWN BETTY.

One cup of bread crumbs, one-half cup of brown sugar, two tablespoons butter, six bananas; put through potato ricer. Fill a buttered baking dish, layer by layer with crumbs and fruit, dot with butter and bake thirty minutes.

BANANA CREAM.

One-half box lemon jello, four bananas, one-fourth cup of sugar, one-half pint of water, one-fourth pint of cream. Pour boiling water on jello, let cool, put bananas through ricer and mix with sugar. Whip cream and blend all ingredients. When lukewarm set on ice in fancy mould. Turn out when set and serve with lady fingers.

FRIED BANANAS.

(Use sweet kind) Slice in half lengths, dip in egg and bread crumbs and fry in deep fat.

Second Receipe—Cook in the fat after cooking ham or bacon for breakfast as you would cold potatoes.

SLICED BANANAS.—Mrs. P. C. Jones.

Take any kind of fully ripe bananas (excepting the plantain), slice quite thin, into a dish, sprinkle a little sugar and grate nutmeg over the top. Let this stand half an hour. Just before taking to the table add cream or milk. Nice for lunch or tea.

BANANA SAUCE.—Miss S. E. Emerson.

A delicious sauce may be made from almost any kind of mellow banana by peeling the fruit, and putting over the fire in a porcelain lined saucepan with a cup of sugar to every seven or eight bananas, also a cup of water. Lemon, orange or tamarind is then to be added to suit the taste.

POI COCKTAIL.

This is the accepted first meal after an attack of seasickness. Beat or shake well together one glass of milk and two tablespoonfuls of poi; flavor with salt, or with nutmeg or sugar, and serve very cold.

GUAVA WHIPS.—Mrs. W. C. Parke.

Take ripe guavas, sweet and sour mixed. Wipe these with a cloth; if not perfectly clean, cut off the ends with a silver knife; mash them well, strain them through any cloth that will allow the juice and pulp to pass through, but not the seeds. Beat into the pulp powdered sugar, about 1 cupful to a pint of the guava. It is difficult to give the exact amount of sugar to be used. It is best to sweeten to taste. Serve in jelly glasses, very cold. (The guava may be strained through a fine hair sieve.—Ed.)

MANGO PUDDING.—Mrs. C. B. Hofgaard.

Two big green mangoes, 2½ cups water, half cup sugar (good measure), half teaspoonful ground cinnamon, 3 tablespoons (heaping) sago. For six people. Method as in Bird Nest Pudding. Page 86.

APPLE SNOW.

Four large sour apples, bake and scrape out the pulp, add half coffee cup of sugar and whites of 2 eggs beaten together until very light. Delicious with cake for dessert or for tea.

MERINGUE OF PAPAIA.—Mrs. Kittredge.

Take the fruit a little under-ripe, steam till quite soft, put through a sieve; then take 2 cups of the sifted papaia, 1 coffee cup sugar, 1 large tablespoonful butter, yolks of 3 eggs, juice of 2 limes and rinds grated. Make a rich butter paste and line 2 pie-plates; put in the mixture and let it bake till the paste is done. While baking, beat the whites of the eggs light and add 1 teacup sifted sugar. Remove the pies from the oven and spread this frosting on them and return to the oven till the frosting is nicely browned.

BAKED PAPAIA.—Mrs. Hiram Bingham.

Take the ripe fruit; halve it and scrape out all the seeds.

Then fill the spaces with good vinegar (lemon or lime juice would probably be nicer if obtainable) and white sugar. Bake until quite soft, and eat hot; or the papaia may be cut in small pieces and mix with acid and sugar, and baked in a deep dish with an upper crust, as a pie.

ORANGE MERINGUE.—Mrs. Hascall.

Five or six oranges, 3 eggs, 1 cup sugar, 1 pint milk, 1 table-spoonful corn starch. Pare the oranges and slice them in a pudding dish, taking care to remove all seeds. Sprinkle the cup of sugar over them, and let them stand while you prepare the following: Heat the milk to boiling and thicken with the corn starch wet with a little cold milk. Let it boil a few minutes, then add the beaten yolks of the eggs. Let the custard cool a few minutes, then pour it over the oranges. Cover this with a meringue of the beaten whites mixed with 2 or 3 table-spoonfuls of powdered sugar. Put it in the oven till of a delicate brown. To be eaten cold. Strawberries are very nice prepared in this way, only taking care to have the custard quite cool when poured over them, that they may be heated as little as possible.

PEACH MERINGUE.—Mrs. Chas. Alexander.

Drain off the syrup from a can of peaches and put them in a pudding dish. Make a soft custard of the yolks of 4 eggs, a quart of milk and 1 teacup of sugar; when cold, pour over the peaches. Beat the whites to a stiff froth, add 5 tablespoonfuls of white sugar and set in the oven to brown.

MANGO MERINGUE.—Mrs. Hascall.

Two or three cups of stewed green mangoes (not too sweet) flavored with lemon or a little nutmeg and poured into a shallow baking dish. Cover with a meringue made of the whites of 3 eggs and 2 tablespoonfus of powdered sugar. Brown slightly, and eat cold for luncheon, or with nice cake for dessert.

A HAWAIIAN FEAST

"AHAAINA," OR MORE COMMONLY CALLED "LUAU."
Mrs. Brickwood and Daughters.

Preparation.—If out in the yard under trees or under an awning, strew the straw or rushes over the place intended for the feast; then spread your mats, ti leaves or la'i in the place of a tablecloth; then ferns on top of that, and then plates, calabashes (wooden bowls) or bowls of poi, and pig, turkey, chicken, raw fish, cooked fish, crabs and limu prepared in various ways.

How the Pig is Prepared and Cooked.—Kill and clean as usual, cut open, then cut under the fore shoulder. In the meantime have your furnace or imu ready and stones heated; take some of the heated stones and put inside the pig (if you wish to stuff, put luau inside); spread ti leaves on the imu and banana leaves on the top of that, and then the pig; cover with the same kind of leaves as are under it; spread over all old mat and then soil. Bake about two hours.

How to Prepare and Cook Salt Pork, Beef, Turkey and Chicken, together or separate.—Heat banana leaves and slice your meat-and put into the leaves, with a little salt sprinkled over it and a little water. If you wish to put luau in with it, put a hot stone in the inside and tie up with ti leaves and put on the furnace. It can be cooked in the same furnace as the pig. Taro can also be cooked in the same place. First scrape the outside off, split in two and place on the fire. When cooked it is called "Kalo papaa," or baked taro.

Luau is the taro tops (or leaves) of three kinds of taro— the Haokea, Lauloa and Apuwai. The young and new leaves are used for eating; the old leaves are sometimes used for wrapping in place of ti leaves or banana leaves.

Cooked or Lawalu Fish.—Take an anae, kuma, weke or any other kind of fish; clean as you would for boiling; take eight or ten ti leaves, sprinkle a little salt, then lay on your fish and wrap your leaves well round it, and put on coals to cook, turning over now and again till cooked. Salt salmon is sometimes cooked in the same way, having first washed off the salt; or it is baked underground.

Kaihelo, or Fish Sauce.—Grate a cocoanut, then take shrimps, sprinkle a little salt on them, pound or bruise them, put in a muslin cloth, and squeeze the juice over the grated cocoanut.

Baked Hee, or Squid.—First pound with a little salt till it shrivels, then rinse out in water and put into banana leaves with ti leaves outside; then bake as the pig.

Wana, or Sea Eggs.—Take the tongues of the wana and put into a large shell and cook on coals.

Roast Kukui Nuts.—Roast your nuts on a slow fire or hot ashes, then when cooked break the shells and pound the meat into small pieces, mixing with a little salt.

Limu, or Sea-weed.—Huluhuluwaena, Lipoa, Limu, Eleele, Limu Kala, Limu Kohu.

PUDDINGS.

Kulolo.—Grate cocoanut and strain, mix with grated taro, add a little water, about a pint of water to a quart of cocoanut juice. A little sugar is sometimes used.   Use 2 taro roots to 5 cocoanuts; put into ti leaves, banana leaves or tin; then bake underground.

Koele Palau.—Sweet potatoes, boiled or baked underground, pounded or mashed; then mix while hot with the juice of some grated cocoanut, and then it is ready for eating.

Piepiele.—Grate the raw sweet potato and add the juice of grated cocoanut, and put into leaves and cook as "Kulolo."

Haupia.—Mix pia or arrowroot with the juice of grated cocoanut.   Heat some of the juice and add to the rest, and stir till cooked, as you would "Blanc Mange."

Papaiee.—Take ripe breadfruit, scrape the inside and mix with a little cocoanut juice, or without; stir till well mixed and put into ti leaves as "Kulolo."

Banana Pudding.—Grate the cocoanut as for Kulolo, put in the banana and mix, adding a little pia or arrowroot.   When mixed put into banana leaves and ti leaves and bake.

SQUASH CAKES.—Mrs. Hascall.

To about 2 cups of cold boiled squash left from dinner, add 2 eggs, 1 tablespoonful sugar, a little salt, 1 tablespoonful butter, 1 small cup milk, ½ teaspoonful soda. Flour to make rather a stiff batter. Fry as griddle cakes.

Updated Version
Serves 4

Ingredients:
2 cups seeded and shredded summer squash
2/3 cup chopped scallions
1 clove of garlic, finely chopped
1 tablespoon chopped fresh rosemary
¼ teaspoon salt
¼ teaspoon pepper
½ Parmesan cheese
1 tablespoon olive oil
2 large eggs

Directions:
Preheat oven to 400 degrees. After shredding squash, place it in a kitchen towel and squeeze tightly to remove all excess liquid. Let it sit while you prepare the other ingredients. In a bowl, lightly beat the eggs and then mix in the scallions, garlic, rosemary, salt, pepper, and cheese. Add the squash to this mixture. Put the oil in a large metal skillet that is ovenproof and turn on medium heat. Pat the squash mixture into four patties and place in the heated oil. Cook for 5 minutes, or until the bottom gets brown, and then flip the patties and place the skillet in the oven to cook for 15 minutes. Serve hot.

The Baptist Cook Book

(1907)

The Baptist Cook Book was published by the Building Fund Association of the First Baptist Church of Albany, Georgia, in 1907. The book was sold to raise funds to replace the wooden church that was built in 1892. In 1911, the wooden building was torn down and construction was begun on the brick sanctuary which still stands today. Due to World War I, construction was not completed until 1918. During that seven-year span, the congregation met in the YMCA building, which was located across the street.

The book is dedicated to "those faithful and much encumbered 'Marthas,' who have, with kind hearts and diligent hands, spread upon the white cloth of its pages, the daintiest and the best of their kitchen knowledge, to furnish a feast for a cause of their Lord, which we happen to represent.

The book's frontispiece features this quote from Ruskin:

Cooking means the knowledge of Medea and Circe and of Helen and of the Queen of Sheba. It means the knowledge of all herbs and fruits and balms and spices and all that is healing and sweet in the field and groves and savory in meats. It means carefulness and inventiveness and willingness and readiness of appliances. It means the economy of your grandmothers and the science of the modern chemist; it means much testing and no wasting; it means English thoroughness and French wit and Arabian hospitality; and in fine, it means that you are to be perfectly and always ladies—loaf-givers."

Those Marthas were quite erudite!

THE

BAPTIST COOK BOOK

Compiled by a Committee from the Building Fund Association
of the First Baptist Church of Albany, Ga., May, 1907.

GILBERT PRINTING CO., COLUMBUS, GA.
1907.

Creole Chicken and Oyster Fillet Gumbo.

One-half of chicken cut as for stew, 2 doz. oysters, 1 tb. of lard to fry, add 1 tb. of flour, 1 onion chopped fine, fry brown; add chicken, fry 15 min., add oyster juice, let boil slowly ½ hr., lastly add oysters with 4 cups of water, let boil 10 min. Before serving dissolve 1 t. of fillet while in the pot.

Note. Crab or shrimp may be used instead of chicken.

MRS. W. G. LAGERQUIST.

Tomato Soup.

Cook for 20 min. 1 can of tomatoes, 1 pt. water, 1 slice of onion, 1 level tb. sugar, 4 cloves, ssp. of white pepper; rub through a strainer, add 3 level tb. of flour, rubbed smooth into tb. of butter, cook 5 min., serve at once.

Gumbo Fillet Powder.

Take very young, tender leaves of sassafras, spread on white paper and dry in a cool, airy place. When dry pound in a morter, press through a seive and keep in a well corked bottle.

C. B.

Bouillon.

Six lbs. of beef soup bone, 1 chicken, slice of ham, an onion, 2 sprigs of parsley, 1 carrot, 1 stick of celery, 3 cloves, pepper and salt, a gallon of cold water. Let beef, chicken and ham boil slowly about 5 hr. Add vegetables and cloves to cook the last hr. Remove from fire and strain into an earthen bowl, let remain over night. Next day remove the fat from the top and take the jelly, without the settlings; put into a kettle, adding the shells and beaten whites of 2 or 3 eggs, let come to a boil 2 or 3 min., skim carefully the eggs and skum from top without stirring the soup. Strain through a thick jelly bag. This soup will keep for days. Reheat before serving. To improve the color add a tb. of caramel which gives a rich amber color.

MRS. A. H. HILSMAN.

Baked Fish.

Take a large fish, nicely cleaned, put in baking pan, and pour over it 2½ c. of water, then put pepper, salt, spice to suit taste; 1 onion and ½ c. butter, bake 30 or 40 min.

Fish au Gratin.

Sheepshead, Red Flounder or Red Snapper, may be used.

Scald, wash, have whole and salt good all over until it falls off, then lay in baking pan. Put on fish in dabs, ½ lb. butter, 3 medium size tomatoes, (sliced) also in pan 1 or 2 lemons same way, then juice of 1 lemon; 1 qt. of French canned mushrooms chopped fine, (leave liquid out) put all over fish; also 2 doz. oysters chopped fine. Pour over all ½ pt. white wine. Put in oven not too hot. Cook ¾ of an hr. To be sure it is ready to serve pass fork into flesh at backbone, and if easily raised it is ready, and if stubborn, cook longer.

MRS. JAMES OSBORN.

Broiled Pompano.

Salt well, butter thick, both sides like you would bread, dust with black pepper, baste while broiling with juice of 1 large lemon. When ready to serve put sliced lemon and parsley over and around the fish.

MRS. JAMES OSBORN.

Deviled Crabs.

Saute' ¼ of a c. of chopped mushroom in 3 tb. of butter 5 min.; sprinkle in 2 tb. of flour, and when blended add ⅔ of a c. of stock. When the mixture boils add a c. of chopped crab meat, a t. of chopped parsley, the beaten yolks of 2 eggs, and season quite high with salt and pepper. Turn the mixture into crab shells trimmed and cleaned, and sprinkle with fine bread crumbs mixed with melted butter. Bake until the crumbs are browned. BOSTON COOKING SCHOOL.

Mince Turnovers.

Two c. flour sifted twice with 1 rounded t. baking powder and ½ as much salt, chop into it 2 tb. butter and wet with cup of sweet milk quickly and lightly. Roll into a sheet less than a ¼ of an inch thick, and cut into squares about 6 inches across, put into middle of each square a large tb. of minced poultry, veal, ham or lamb, or a mixture of these, well seasoned, with gravy; double the paste into a triangle and enfolding the meat, pinch edges firmly to hold together and bake. They are good hot or cold. Mrs. E. H. Muse.

Mint Sauce.

Juice of 2 lemons, 5 scant t. of sugar, 1 tb. of salt, desired quantity of mint, cut fine. Serve with lamb roast.

Mrs. Lee Dees.

Beef or Mutton Souffle.

Two c. cold ground meat, 6 eggs beaten separately, 1 c. milk, 2 tb. butter; put in baking-dish, cook. Serve hot.

Mrs. D. F. Crossland.

Meat Roll.

One uncooked chicken, cut from the bone, 1 lb. round steak, 1 lb. fresh pork; grind together; 2 eggs, ½ c. bread crumbs; season to taste with red and black pepper, a bit of sage and salt. Make in a roll the size of a loaf of bread; put in pan; pour over it 1 c. of boiling water; sprinkle with bread crumbs; lay strips of breakfast bacon on top when nearly done; bake 1 hr., basting often. Mrs. George W. Brown.

Baked Hash.

One qt. cold cooked meat, chopped fine; 1 pt. chopped, uncooked potatoes; 2 eggs, salt and pepper to taste. Put chopped potatoes in a stew-pan with 1 pt. of water; let them stew 5 min.; then add the meat and enough water to make the mixture moist; stew 10 min. longer. Take from the fire; add eggs, beaten; the salt and pepper; turn in baking-dish and bake in quick oven. Mrs. L. F. Allen.

Hot Tamales.

Three lb. choice beef, 1 lb. pork, boiled tender; 6 large pods Chili pepper, (remove seed and boil until soft) 2 pods garlic, ¼ t. cammenie seed, ¼ t. Mexican sage, 1 t. black pepper, 2 tb. salt, 1 c. lard.   Grind all together.   ½ gal. country meal, 1 tb. salt, 1 c. of lard; mix with cold water to thickness of paste, spread a heaping t. of this on shuck, then put in ground meat, roll.   Put in dinner pot and cover with cold water; cook 45 min. over slow fire.   To prepare shucks cut ends off and scald.

MAGGIE.

To Roast a Turkey.

Make a dough of 1 qt. of flour, a pinch of salt; mix with water.   Kill turkey the day before, and salt.   Place turkey in baking-pan half full of water; roll out the dough and cover the turkey with the dough, being careful to tuck under all around, and bake 3 hrs.   MRS. J. T. COOPER.

Brain Patties.

For 12 patties put 2 sets of brains and 1 can of mushrooms; boil the brains done.   Take off and put in clear water and lemon juice.   Chop fine mushrooms and brains together, add 1 tb. of butter, ½ c. of cream, add pepper, white and red to taste, 1 t. finely chopped parsley, a grating of nutmeg, put in a ramekin.   Grate bread crumbs on top and brown in oven. Serve hot.   MRS. ANNA TAYLOR.

Turkey Croquettes.

To 1 pt. of minced turkey add ¼ c. of bread crumbs, 2 eggs and sufficient gravy to moisten all.   Season to taste and mix well.   Flour the hands and make into croquettes.   Dip in beaten egg; then into bread crumbs, and fry a delicate brown.

MRS. W. I. CHERRY.

Stuffed Cabbage.

Use a head of white cabbage; remove carefully ½ doz. of the outer leaves, cut a good sized circle in the top with a sharp knife; reserve a few pieces cut off the top, and then remove the inside of the cabbage, leaving only a frame; be very careful not to cut into it, or the dressing will escape. Now, put the frame in salted water and boil 10 min.; chop the inside of the cabbage into small bits; put in cold water and boil until tender; soak ¼ of a loaf of bread in cold water; squeeze out all the water; add ¼ lb. of pork; put on a fryer with 2 tb. butter; when hot, put in the soaked bread and cooked cabbage; fry until it leaves the side of the fryer; remove to a bowl; season with salt, pepper and ginger. Add 2 eggs, mix well, fill in the cabbage; put on the top, tie the outside leaves around and bake.

Mrs. B. S.

Stuffed Tomatoes.

Cut a slice from the stem ends of the tomatoes, scoop out the seeds and a portion of the hard centers; to each 6 good sized tomatoes allow a pt. bread crumbs, a tb. chopped parsley, a tb. of grated onion, a level t. of salt, a ssp. of pepper and 2 tb. of melted butter; mix, stuff this in the tomatoes, heaping it slightly, stand them in baking pan, add ½ cup water and bake in slow oven ¾ hr., basting once or twice with little melted butter.

R. N.

Dried Peas.

One pt. peas, picked over and soaked in water from 1 to 2 hrs.; drain and cover with cold water and boil until tender. In another vessel boil a small piece of salt pork; when the peas are thoroughly done, drain off all water and pour them into the vessel with the meat, adding more hot water, if necessary; boil about 30 min. longer and they are ready to serve.

R. N.

Angels Charlotte Russe.

One tb. Knox gelatine, ¼ c. cold water, ¼ c. boiling water, 1 c. sugar, 1 pt. sweet cream, 1 doz. marshmallows. Soak gelatine in cold water 10 min., then dissolve in hot water and add sugar. When mixture is cold add cream. Beat until stiff, and add the marshmallows which have been cut in small pieces. Flavor with vanilla or sherry wine, and garnish with candied cherries when served. To the above recipe may be added ½ doz. stale maccaroons, ¼ lb. blanched and chopped almonds, and 2 tb. chopped candied cherries (in which case dispense with whole cherries as a garnish).

Mrs. C. B. James.

White Charlotte Russe with Fruit.

One qt. cream, 1 lb. sugar, ½ box of Cox's gelatine, 1 wine glass wine, 1 t. vanilla, whites of 6 eggs, ½ lb. crystalized cherries, 2 rounds of crystalized pineapple, both cut fine; 1 c. of chopped almonds. Add part of the sugar to cream and whip to a stiff froth. Whip eggs stiff; add remaining sugar to them, then whip them into the cream; beat well and flavor. Lastly, add the gelatine after it has been dissolved into ½ c. of water. Whip all together, then add the fruit.

Mrs. J. D. Armstrong.

Fruit-Salpicon (Sweet).

Three bananas, 2 oranges or a pt. of strawberries, ½ pine-apple, ½ c. Maraschino cherries, juice of 1 lemon, 1 c. sugar, ½ lb. white grapes. Peel bananas, remove coarse threads and slice. Peel oranges, seed, and cut in slices. Peel pineapple and with fork pull off fruit from the core. Skin the grapes and take out seed and cut in 2 parts. If the strawberries are used cut in half. Mix the fruit lightly with sugar and lemon juice and chill thoroughly and quickly. Serve in sherbert cups with whipped cream as a sweet dish at the close of dinner, or without cream, as a relish, at the beginning of luncheon party.

Mrs. J. W. Walters.

Peach Short-cake.

Make B. P. biscuit dough, sweeten slightly, cut out 2 large rounds ½ in. thick; put one on the other, with soft butter between, and bake.   Separate layers and spread the lower one with peaches, sweetened and crushed; lay on top layer and sprinkle with powdered sugar, and arrange a circle of halved peaches all around the edge.   Serve with cream.

MRS. MUNNERLYN.

Trifle.

One layer of sliced sponge-cake in a dish, 1 layer of syllabub quite strong with sherry, 1 layer of boiled custard, 1 layer of *small* pieces of jelly, 1 layer of sliced almonds which have been peeled by dropping them in hot water and rubbing the outside skin off, and broken up in small pieces, 1 layer of raisins, *after taking skins off*.   Repeat these layers until the dish is full, and put syllabub on top.

MRS. CLARK HOWELL.

Apple Foam.

Pare and quarter ripe, juicy apples to fill a pt. cup; to 1 pt. water and 1 c. sugar add the apples and cook until tender, without breaking.   Mix 3 tb. corn starch in little cold water, add to apples, stirring constantly; cook 5 min., turn into a mold, previously dipped in cold water and set away to cool. Serve with whipped cream.

Pineapple Ambrosia.

One pt. ripe strawberries, 1 pt. chopped pineapple, 1 pt. of cream (whip cream stiff), place a layer of pineapple in a glass dish, sprinkle with sugar, cover with whipped cream, then with a layer of the berries, continue these layers until the dish is full; heap the sugar on top and serve very cold with sponge cake.

Rice Pudding.

One-half c. cooked rice, 2 eggs, 1 c. sugar, 1 qt. milk, ½ cup chopped and seeded raisins, pinch of salt; flavor with nutmeg.

Mrs. J. R. Whitehead.

Christmas Pudding.

Slice a loaf of stale bread and spread with plenty of butter, 1 layer of bread close together in pan, sprinkle liberally with fruit, currants and raisins, then another layer of buttered bread and fruit until the pan is 1 inch of oeing full. Make a custard out of 1 qt. of milk and 4 eggs; sweeten to taste. Pour over contents of pan and let it set over night, next morning make another custard ½ the quantity and pour over. Set pan in oven immediately after breakfast and bake 4 or 5 hr. When pudding browns set plate over to keep from burning. Serve with butter sauce.

Mrs. S. E. Campbell.

Chocolate Pudding.

Four c. milk, 4 tb. corn starch, 4 tb. grated chocolate, ¾ c. sugar, 1 egg. Boil milk, stir in corn starch after being wet with a little water; add to beaten eggs sugar and chocolate, boil till thick; pour into cups that have been wet with cold water and serve with whipped cream. Whip 1 c. of cream sweetened to taste and flavor with vanilla.

Caramel Pudding.

Four eggs, 1 c. sugar, 1 c. butter, 1 c. jelly or preserves, 1 tb. vanilla; eggs beaten separately. Make merangue.

Blackberry Sponge.

Fill an earthen bowl closely with small cubes of bread, pouring over the bread as it is fitted into place hot blackberry juice; blackberries cooked until soft, with sugar to taste, and pass through a seive; use all the juice the bread will absorb; set the sponge aside in a cool place for some hrs.; then turn from the bowl and serve with blackberries, sugar and cream.

Hickory Nut Macaroons.

One pt. granulated sugar, 4 eggs, 1 pt. flour, 1 pt. of kernels, stir together and drop on a buttered flat tin; bake slowly for 20 minutes.   Mrs. W. W. Rawlings.

Peanut Macaroons.

Mix 1 c. of finely chopped peanuts, 1 c. of sifted confectioners sugar, 1 large tb. of flour, and make into a stiff paste with the unbeaten whites of 2 eggs; drop upon buttered pans, allowing room to spread, and bake in a moderate oven.

Mrs. H. A. Floyed.

Almond Wafers.

Cream ½ c. butter, add gradually 1 c. powdered sugar, and then drop by drop ½ c. milk, and lastly 2 c. pastry flour and ½ t. vanilla extract. Spread very thin on the bottom of baking pans, inverted and buttered. Mark in squares, sprinkle with almonds, blanched and chopped fine; bake in a slow oven about 5 min. Cut the wafers apart at the marking and roll at once, while warm, either in tubular or cornucopia shape. Before rolling, turn the wafers to bring the nuts on the outside.

Mrs. Wm. Lockett.

Cocoanut Drops.

Take the beaten whites of 2 eggs and stir in equal parts of dessicated cocoanut and powdered sugar until it forms a thick paste; shape into balls and bake on buttered paper until a pale brown.

Mrs. W. W. Rawlings.

Peanut Wafers.

Take ¼ c. butter, ½ c. pulverized sugar, ¾ c. milk, 1 c. flour, ½ c. chopped peanuts. Beat sugar and butter together; stir in milk; add flour by degrees; rub flat pans with beeswax; when cold, spread with thin cakes; sprinkle top with peanuts and bake.

Mrs. J. B. Gilbert.

INVALID DIET.

Scraped Beef.

This is simply beef from which all indigestible substances have been removed. Take a tender piece of beef, cut across the grain, scrape with a spoon until all the pulp is removed; make a fresh surface by cutting off the scraped part with a thin, sharp knife; proceed in this way until all the meat is reduced to a pulp. If necessary, it may be eaten raw, spread very thin on slices of toast, or the pulp may be put in a hot fryingpan with a little butter and allowed to barely cook through, stirring and turning constantly. A weak stomach will often retain scraped beef when it refuses all other solid foods.

MRS. H. A. FLOYD.

Steak on Toast.

Toast slices of bread, grind raw meat, spread on bread with butter, pepper and salt. Put in stove and bake till meat is cooked. MRS. GEO. BROWN.

Egg Lemonade.

One egg, beat. Add 3 tb. lemon juice, beat; add 3 tb. sugar, beat; add 1 c. milk, hot or cold. MRS. G. W.

Orange Whey.

The juice of 1 orange to 1 pt. sweet milk. Heat slowly until curd forms, strain and cool. Good drink for the sick.

MRS. A. B. S.

Beef Essence.

Take a nice round steak and pound it thoroughly and broil on a hot griddle with little butter just half done, then cut in convenient pieces and put in lemon squeezer and press out the juice in tea cup, having the cup warm; season with a little salt and pepper. A good and mild stimulant for the sick.

PLANTENE is a perfect substitute for either hog lard or butter; use about one-half the quantity of "Plantene" as of either. Observe directions on can.

Vegetable Pudding.

Boil a firm white cabbage 15 mins., changing water; when tender remove, drain, let cool, chop fine, add 2 beaten eggs, 1 tb. butter, 3 tb. rich milk or cream, pepper and salt; stir all well together; bake in a buttered pudding dish until brown; serve hot. This dish is easily digested, palatable and tasts much like cauliflower.   MARY PATTESON.

Updated Version

1 head of cabbage
2 ½ quarts of water
Six slices of turkey bacon
1 teaspoon crushed red pepper
2 cups of milk
3 eggs
1 teaspoon salt
1 tablespoon mustard of your choice

Pinch of cayenne pepper
Pinch of black pepper
1 cup of cubed bread
½ teaspoon basil
½ teaspoon thyme
¼ cup bread crumbs
2 tablespoons of melted butter

Directions:

Preheat oven to 350 degrees. Put the water, red pepper flakes, and bacon in a pot and bring to a boil. Cut the cabbage into quarters and boil for 15 minutes. Drain the cabbage and bacon, chop them up and place in a bowl. In another bowl, mix the milk, eggs, salt, mustard, and peppers. Pour this mixture over the cabbage and bacon and mix again. Toss the bread cubes with the herbs and press into the bottom of a large baking dish or pan that has been greased. Pour the cabbage mixture over the bread cubes, and top with the bread crumbs. Drizzle the melted butter on last, and bake for 60 minutes. Serves 6.

Westminster Church
Cook Book

(1916)

The first Westminster Church (see below) was completed in 1866 and was located at 6th and L Streets in downtown Sacramento, California. The folks pictured below at the annual Sunday School picnic (1910) are probably about to feast on the results of the recipes in this book.

DEVILED CRAB.

Pick and mince crab; one cup milk, two spoonfuls Globe A-1 flour cooked smooth, two table spoonfuls butter, one small mustard spoonful mustard; stir in two table spoonfuls bread crumbs, one-half lemon juice; salt and pepper to taste; add yolk of two eggs, hard boiled, chopped fine; put in shell, cover with bits of butter, and bake.—Myra P. Miller.

CREOLE OF CRAB.

Four green peppers, six small green onions, chop fine; add butter the size of an egg, and salt and pepper to taste; boil ten minutes, then add one-half can tomatoes and boil until all is well dissolved; add one-half pint of cream, mix with one tablespoonful of Globe A-1 flour and let come to a boil; pour in two well picked crabs, and serve on toast.—Mrs. Charles Gross.

CRABS, HARD SHELL, SAUTED.

One cup boiled crab meat; three tablespoons butter; juice of half a lemon; salt and paprica; after seasoning the crab meat with lemon juice, salt and paprica, saute in hot melted butter.

CRAB LOUIS.

Rub dish with garlic, then add one-half cup tomato catsup, two table-spoons olive oil, three tablespoons vinegar, a little paprica, one teaspoon salt, one Worcestershire sauce, two hard boiled eggs sliced fine; pour over cracked crab, properly iced, and lettuce leaves.

OYSTER SCOLLOPED.

Oysters, two tablespoons cracker dust or cracker crumbs, one gill cream, two tablespoons butter, pepper, salt; put the butter and cream into chafing dish; after draining, put in oysters in layers, sprinkle with cracker crumbs; a little seasoning to taste; cover and cook from five to ten minutes.

MINCED FISH.

One quart cold fish carefully flaked, one pint of milk or cream, one can of mushrooms cut in halves, two tablespoons of butter, two table-spoons of Globe A-1 flour; put butter in frying pan to melt, then add milk or cream; stir continually until it boils; add mushrooms and liquor and pour this over the minced fish and mix carefully; salt and pepper to taste; put all in a pan and grate cheese on the top; place in an oven and let brown.

SALMON SOUFFLE.

Make thick white sauce, add one teacup rolled cracker crumbs, onion juice, one teaspoon chopped parsley, Worcestershire sauce, dash of catsup, can of salmon, heat thoroughly, beaten yolks of two eggs, beaten whites folded in; cook in casserole or ramekins twenty-five minutes.

STUFFING FOR BAKED FISH.

One cup cracker crumbs, one teaspoonful salt, one teaspoonful pepper, one teaspoonful chopped onion, one teaspoonful chopped parsley, one tea-spoonful capers, one teaspoonful pickles, one-fourth cup of melted butter. Cook onions, parsley in melted butter; season Paprika, Worcestershire sauce; stir in the rest.

SAUCE FOR FISH.

Egg Sauce—Boil three or four eggs hard; cut them fine and stir into drawn butter. If too thick, add a little cream or rich milk.

HOLLANDAISE SAUCE FOR BAKED OR BOILED FISH.

One cup butter, yolks of two eggs, juice of one-half lemon, one salt-spoon salt, one-quarter saltspoon cayenne, one-half cup boiling water. Rub butter to a cream in small bowl with wooden or silver spoon, add yolks one at a time and beat; add salt, pepper, lemon juice. Place bowl in a sauce pan of boiling water, stir rapidly until it thickens like boiled custard; pour over meat or fish.

HALLIBUT SUFFLE.

Boil a pint or a pound of any kind of fish (hallibut preferred), left overs will do. Shred or mash to a pulp; add one teaspoonful salt, dash of pepper, one teaspoonful onion juice. Melt a heaping tablespoonful of butter and to it add one tablespoonful Globe A-1 flour and cook to a paste. To this add slowly one cup milk then the fish and two well beaten eggs. Bake one-half hour in buttered pan.—Mrs. Nicholas H. Bath.

OYSTER STUFFING.

One-half a cup each of cracker and bread crumbs, one-fourth cup of butter, one-half pint of oysters, two tablespoonfuls lemon juice, one-half tablespoonful chopped parsley, oyster liquor to moisten and salt and pepper. Mrs. A. J. Gibson.

CREAMED LOBSTER.

One onion minced fine; simmer in tablespoon butter, heaping table-spoon Globe A-1 flour added; then add cup of cream, pinch of soda in cream, two teaspoons catsup, one dash tobasco and one teaspoon Worcestershire sauce. Chop lobster not too fine and add to sauce; put grated cheese on top and bake twenty minutes.

SAUCE FOR LOBSTER CREOLE.

One can tomatoes (Del Monte Sauce), simmer one-half hour with one large onion and clove of garlic minced; strain. Cook one large tablespoon of Globe A-1 flour and butter until blended, add the tomato, and after it boils up add slowly one-half cup cream, one-half teaspoon each chili powder and Grandma's Spanish pepper, one tablespoon grated Italian cheese. You may add hard boiled eggs sliced, or stoned olives. Pour this over diced lobster and serve hot.

LOBSTER A'LA NEWBERG.

Split two good sized lobsters, pick meat from shells and dice; place in a saucepan with a good lump of butter, season with salt and red pepper and one-half can mushrooms diced; cook five minutes, then add a wine glass of Madiera wine. Have three eggs and one-half pint of cream beaten together; add to the lobster and cook until it thickens.

ENTREES

"The turnpike to people's hearts, I find
Lies through their mouths, or I mistake mankind."

CHEESE SOUFFLE— (Delicious).

One cup grated cheese, one egg, one teaspoon thick cream, one-quarter teaspoon mustard; salt, pepper and paprika to taste. Melt cheese, add cream, salt, pepper and paprika; let cool; add yolk, then beaten white of egg. Butter ramekins and put small piece of bread in bottom of them. Fill with mixture three-quarters full, bake ten to fifteen minutes.—E. N. P.

CHEESE FONDU.

One cup fresh bread crumbs, two cups grated cheese, one cup milk, spoonful soda, one-half teaspoonful salt, spoonful red pepper, one table-spoonful butter, two eggs. Put butter in sauce pan to heat while you beat the eggs light without separating them. Let these stand while you stir everything else into the pan, beginning with the milk. Cook this five minutes, stirring all the time. Put in eggs and cook three minutes more. Place crackers on hot platter and pour the whole over them.—E. S.

ENGLISH MONKEY.

One tablespoon melted butter, one cup fine stale bread crumbs, two cups cheese cut in small squares, one cup milk. Put all these ingredients into a sauce pan, stir until cheese is melted; if too thick, add more milk; season to taste with salt, paprika and Worcestershire; then add two well beaten eggs. Do not cook after eggs have been added. Serve on hot crackers.—M. G. K.

WELSH RARBIT.

Quarter pound of grated cheese, one tablespoonful butter, the yolk of one egg well beaten with two tablespoonfuls of milk; little salt, pepper and mustard. Stir until melted and pour on toasted slices of bread.—J. W. W.

ENCHILADAS.

Mix a stiff dough of three cups Globe A-1 flour, one cup cold water and teaspoon salt. Roll very thin and bake on top of range in cakes size of pie tin. Dip each enchilada in thick Spanish sauce; then cover quickly with grated cheese with which a chopped onion and three chopped hard boiled eggs have been mixed. Roll each enchilada and place in a thick earthen platter in moderate oven ten minutes.—C. G.

CORN TAMALES.

One can corn, one cup tomatoes, three-quarters cup corn meal, one and one-half cups milk, chopped green pepper, onion, few olives, one teaspoon Grandma's Spanish pepper, one teaspoon salt. Put in buttered baking dish and bake three-quarters or one hour. Bake slowly.—B. T. W.

CHEESE SOUFFLE.

One cup milk, one cup cheese, grated, three eggs, one tablespoon Globe A-1 flour, two tablespoons butter. Rub butter, flour and warm milk together; beat eggs in one at a time. Cook in a double boiler, add cheese, beat whites in and bake one-half hour in moderate oven in ramekins.—Mrs. C. H.

HAM, SOUTHERN STYLE.

Put ham on to boil, cooking slowly; when done, let cool in the water; when cool, remove skin, gash top with a knife, sprinkle on this two teaspoons of sugar, a little dry mustard, one teaspoon celery, salt, cracker crumbs, wine glass of sherry, and put in over and bake a few minutes; garnish with parsley.—K. M. H.

BOILED HAM.

Boil ham (or half a ham) three hours with bay leaf. Leave in water all night. Skin it and rub all over with sugar. Sprinkle fat part with bread crumbs and stick it full of cloves. Bake one-half hour; baste with sherry or champagne.

SWEET BREADS.

Parboil one and one-half pounds sweet breads, cut rather fine, chop together one-half can mushrooms. Put two tablespoons of butter in frying pan, add one onion, fry light brown. Add sweet breads and stir until brown. Add one small cup sherry, salt and pepper to taste. Place cover on pan and simmer slowly for fifteen minutes. If too wet remove cover and dry; if too dry add a little cream.

POTATO CRUST FOR MEAT PIES.

One cup potatoes mashed, two cups flour, one teaspoon salt, two teaspoons yeast powder, half cup shortening, milk to make soft dough.—A. K.

CHICKEN TAMALES.

Boil tow chickens, save liquor; chop chickens coarsely; mix with four hard boiled eggs and twenty-five cents worth tamale paste. To thirty cents worth of cooked hominy put through grinder add two raw eggs, melted butter, salt and pepper. Line dishes with this and fill with chicken; steam one hour.—A. K.

ROAST FILLET.

Roast in hot oven; for each pound of meat allow twenty minutes; baste frequently, add salt and pepper while roasting. When done take out fillet, add one tablespoon Globe A-1 flour to gravy, one can mushrooms sliced, small glass of sherry; pour sauce around the meat sliced one inch thick.—Mrs. W. J. T.

JELLIED MEAT.

Take teal or chicken—To two chickens, two onions, six cloves, six whole white peppers, two bay leaves, one blade of mace, four whole allspice, one-half cup vinegar, salt to taste, one lemon, one and one-half box of gelatine, two quarts water. Put chicken on to boil with salt and water; skim well, then add onions, cloves, etc., and boil until meat drops from bones; strain, let stock get cool and remove fat; cut chicken into small pieces, put jelly on and bring to boil. Put meat into a dish or molds and pour the jelly over hot; add vinegar and lemon to jelly just before pouring over meat.—Mrs. A. M. Stevenson.

POT ROAST.

For $1 roast—Flour, salt and pepper roast well; slice one large onion and brown with one tablespoon of Globe A-1 flour in butter; use small pan. In deep pot place four tablespoons of butter and same amount of lard; when hot put roast in and brown on each side; add browned onion, one scraped carrot, one celery root cut in four pieces; half cover the roast with water and let it steam two and one-half hours.—H. A. H.

CHICKEN ASPARAGUS.

Boil one chicken tender and cut in dice shape; one can of asparagus, tender parts only; make a sauce of one quart of cream, tablespoonful of Globe A-1 flour, juice of one lemon, salt and pepper. Pour this over the chicken and asparagus, first having put it in individual plates; grate a little cheese on top and bake fifteen minutes in ramekins. Splendid for afternoon tea.—Mrs. J. W. Stett.

BRAIN TUMBOLIS.

For fifteen cents worth of brains take two large slices bread soaked in milk, beat four eggs, add brains and bread, season with salt, pepper, pinch ginger, paprica and Worcestershire sauce. Steam three-quarters of an hour.

SAUCE.

One tablespoon butter mix with one tablespoon Globe A-1 flour, add one-half pint cream, salt, paprica, juice of one lemon, little nutmeg; add two tablespoons catsup and one-half can mushrooms.—Mrs. P. B. Ward.

BRAIN TIMBALS.

Fifteen cents worth of brains soaked in salt water and strained; two slices of bread soaked in milk; squeeze milk out and mix with brains; beat yolks of four eggs and mix with bread and brains; beat whites and season with salt, pepper and Worcestershire sauce. Steam three-quarters of an hour; serve with cream sauce, season with catsup, mushrooms and oysters; butter tins.—Mrs. C. H.

ITALIAN DISH.

One pound of pork sausage meat, one and one-half cup macaroni, one green pepper chopped, one onion chopped, six tomatoes cut. Put meat sausage in stew pan with a cup of water; add pepper, onion and tomatoes and cook one hour over a slow fire; boil macaroni in salt water; when done drain, put on platter and grate cheese on macaroni, then pour meat over. Put on meat a little cinnamon and cloves.—Mrs. Whitman.

"MULLIGAN."

Take two pounds of round steak and cut into pieces two inches square; dredge well with Globe A-1 flour; cut up one large onion and brown it in drippings, then remove the onion and brown the steak. Put in sauce pan and cover with boiling water. Add one-half can of tomatoes and two small green peppers cut into small pieces, one bay leaf. Boil very slowly for about three hours. Season with salt, pepper, tobasco and Worcestershire sauce. Thicken if necessary.

CURRY, FROM ORIGINAL INDIA RECEIPT.

Procure lamb or young mutton from shoulder. Cut in pieces about twice as thick as the usual chop and then cut in pieces about two inches. Heat beef drippings boiling hot in thick pot or frying pan. Put in the meat and brown it. Then to twenty-five cents worth of meat take one tablespoon of curry powder, sprinkle over meat while it is browning, letting it come in contact with every part. Care must be taken not to scorch the curry or flavor will be spoiled. Add water to cover, one green onion, one fried onion, a carrot cut in thick slices, a little parsley, and potatoes on top. Salt to taste. Allow to cook two hours. Before serving remove potatoes and thicken with Globe A-I flour. Serve boiled rice with this dish. —K. M. H.

REAL ENGLISH CURRIE.

Stew twenty-five cents worth of lamb twenty minutes. Brown two onions and two apples (after you have chopped them fine) in a little bacon grease, add a pinch of salt, two dessertspoonfuls of currie; then mix it all in the lamb stew, cook for two hours; just before serving add two tablespoonfuls of Globe A-1 flour and a little lemon juice. Serve with rice.

GYPSY STEW.

One and one-half pounds round steak or veal, ground; one bunch celery; boiling water to cover, and stew until tender; add salt and pepper to taste; three-quarters cup of grated cheese; one-half cup English walnuts; one cup milk, and thicken with two pounds Globe A-1 flour. Garnish with toast points.

CHARTREUSE OF MUTTON.

Take two quarts of boiling water, one cup of rice and two teaspoonfuls salt and cook until done. Now mix two cups cold cooked chopped mutton, two eggs slightly beaten, two teaspoonfuls of finely chopped parsley, one teaspoonful lemon juice, one teaspoonful of onion juice, one fourth teaspoonful of salt and black and red pepper. Butter mold, line bottom and sides with rice, fill in seasoned meat, cover with rice, tie on buttered paper and steam forty minutes. When done turn out on a platter and serve with tomato sauce. Left overs of any kind of meat can be used in the same way.

YORKSHIRE PUDDING.

(Serve with Hot Roast Beef—English Style.)

Three eggs, broken into two cups of Globe A-1 flour, into which two teaspoons of baking powder and one teaspoon of salt have been sifted. Beat into these ingredients one pint of milk, making a smooth batter, about the consistency of rich cream. Remove the roast from pan, and, after draining off most of the drippings, pour in the batter. Raise meat on a skeleton stand so that it rests above, but not on the batter, and the drippings from the meat can fall on the pudding. Cook in moderate oven about one-half hour, and serve in slices with the meat.—K. M. H.

Just a Hint.

When browning a pot roast add a tablespoon of sugar to the fat. It produces a beautiful brown and a delicious flavor.—K. M. H.

BAKED EGG PLANT.

Boil about twenty minutes; take inside out, add two spoonfuls of cheese, two cloves garlic, one egg, two spoonfuls oil; salt; mix all these and then bake with cheese and oil in pan.—J. B.

STUFFED CABBAGE.

Cook a medium-sized cabbage about fifteen minutes, until its leaves can be turned back and opened up like a rose; sprinkle minced cold boiled ham (home boiled preferred) which has been mixed with a little olive oil, between each leaf; fold leaves together again, tie in cheese cloth and steam from one to two hours, according to size of cabbage. Serve hot or cold and slice to serve it.—H. A.

BAKED CORN—SPANISH.

Put one can of corn into a large bowl, add one cup of milk, one cup of white cornmeal, two well beaten eggs. Prepare for food chopper, six medium-sized tomatoes (or about one pint of canned), two bell peppers, two or three onions (according to size), a dose of garlic if liked, cut very fine. Add this ground mixture to corn: One tablespoon "Grandma's Peppers" (ground chili), two tablespoons of olive oil, one large cup or more of green olives; salt and pepper to taste. Mix well and put in earthen baking dishes; cook in oven slowly for about an hour or till thoroughly cooked. Do not fill dishes to the top, for it swells in cooking. Very good with cold chicken. Fill two medium-sized dishes. This may be prepared with hamburg steak instead of the corn— leave out the olives. It is then "Vienna Loaf."—M. H. L.

SPANISH RICE.

Cook rice in double boiler, one cup to three or four persons; one tablespoon ham or bacon fat, add onion and green pepper and fry slightly; add four tomatoes and cook slowly until mixture is smooth; season with salt, pepper and a little allspice. When dressing is done pour over rice and mix thoroughly before covering with grated cheese.— B. G. W.

COLACHI (SPANISH).

Take two or three summer squash, the yellow crook-neck ones are the best; one large onion, two green peppers and three or four ripe tomatoes (peeled); chop fine in a bowl and season; put in a frying pan some good dripping, and when hot add the chopped vegetables and cook slowly one hour or more.—C. G.

SPANISH ONIONS.

Take as many onions as you wish to bake; remove the hearts and put in a chopping bowl with a few pieces of cooked meat, one green pepper, salt and black pepper; chop fine and fry brown; then fill onions with this mixture, put a small piece of butter on each and bake; when done pour a sauce made from red chili peppers over all, and return to oven a few minutes.

CARROT PUDDING.

One cupful chopped suet, one cupful Globe A-1 flour, one cupful bread crumbs, one cupful grated raw potatoes, one cupful grated raw carrots, two cupfuls raisins, one-half cupful syrup, one-half cupful milk, one-half teaspoonful Hallifax Quality baking powder (use less of this powder than other powders). Boil in mold for four hours. Serve with wine or hard sauce or beaten egg sauce.

SWEET POTATO PUDDING.

Two cupfuls of grated sweet potatoes. Beat cupful of sugar into four eggs very light. One-half cupful of butter, nutmeg or spices to taste. Bake in an earthen dish for about an hour and a half and serve with hard sauce.

IMPERIAL PUDDING.

One-fourth cupful of rice, one cupful of milk, one-half cupful of sugar, two tablespoonsful of mace or flavor with vanilla, one-half teaspoonful of salt, one-fourth box of gelatine soaked in one-fourth cup of cold water. Put rice to boil in one pint of cold water. As soon as hot pour off all the water; add the milk; boil one hour in double boiler; add gelatine, sugar, salt and flavoring; when cold add one cup of whipped cream or serve with custard made of one-half cupful of sugar, one pint milk and two eggs.

ZABAJOUE.

(Portion for one person.) Yolk of one egg, one-half egg shell of sugar, one-half egg shell sherry, one teaspoonful Maraschino. Put in double boiler and place over fire; stir constantly until consistency of whipped cream. Remove immediately and add one tablespoonful of whipped cream. Put in glass to cool. Serve ice cold.

PLUM PUDDING.

One-half pound suet chopped fine, little salt, one pound seeded raisins, one pound currants, one-quarter citron and lemon peel, one pound bread crumbs, six eggs, one cup milk, one teaspoon allspice, one-fourth teaspoon cloves, two teaspoon cinnamon, one pound sugar, one wine glass brandy, add one cup chopped almonds. Boil six hours—the longer the better.—A. K.

PINEAPPLE BAVARIAN CREAM.

One can grated pineapple, one cup sugar, one-half box gelatine, one-half cup cold water, one-half cup boiling water, one pint cream. Stew pineapple and sugar together ten minutes; soak gelatine in cold water until soft and dissolve in boiling water; strain into pineapple and cool; add cream well whipped and set away in mould.—C. M. C.

DELICIOUS RICE DESSERT.

One-half cup boiled rice, one pint boiled custard, one cup preserved strawberries. Put these in a dessert dish, first the rice, then the custard and then the berries; cover with whipped cream. Ramekin dishes may be used instead of one large dish.—C. M. C.

SHRIMP WIGGLE—(Fine).

One cup of shrimps (canned or fresh), one cup of peas (cooked), one-eighth teaspoon paprika, one large tablespoon Globe A-1 flour, one and one-half cups milk, two tablespoons butter, one teaspoon salt, one teaspoon chopped parsley. Prepare the shrimps by rinsing, draining and breaking in small pieces; soften the butter in pan, mix the Globe A-1 flour well with it, then pour on gradually the milk, and as soon as the sauce thickens add the shrimps and peas with all the seasonings; bring to the boiling point and serve on buttered soda crackers. This will serve eight people.— Mrs. C. Cunningham.

Updated Version

Ingredients:
1 pound fresh shrimp, peeled, or frozen shrimp, thawed and peeled
4 tablespoons butter
2 tablespoons flour
2 tablespoons lemon juice
½ teaspoon dry mustard
1¼ cup milk
½ teaspoon Worchestershire sauce
Salt and pepper
1½ cups frozen peas

Directions:
Melt butter in a large skillet, then add shrimp and lemon juice. Cook until shrimp is no longer pink. Remove the shrimp and set aside. Put the flour and dry mustard in the skillet and mix until smooth. Pour in the milk and bring to a boil, stirring constantly. Add the Worchestershire sauce, and salt and pepper to taste. Add the frozen peas and again bring to a boil. Put the shrimp back in the skillet and mix well before serving. This dish can be served as an appetizer or a main course. You can ladle it over rice or pasta, or put it in puff pastry shells.

The Housekeeper's Friend

(1876)

The Housekeeper's Friend was published in 1876 to raise funds for the Zanesville, Ohio, Home of the Friendless (i.e., the poorhouse), "an institution most worthy of the patronage of all benevolent people." It was written by "A Lady of Zanesville," identified only by her initials, J. W. B., who hoped that "the work will find favor in the eyes of the public (if not for its own merits) for the noble cause it represents."

In addition to its many wonderful (and sometimes, quaint) recipes, this invaluable book contains tips on how to clean your house and body, remove freckles, and even cure cancer and cholera (see page 171 of this book; disclaimer—the editors do not recommend this).

THE HOUSEKEEPER'S FRIEND:

A PRACTICAL COOK-BOOK,

COMPILED BY

A LADY OF ZANESVILLE,

AND SOLD FOR THE

Benefit of the Home of the Friendless.

———

"Behold! his breakfasts shine with reputation;
His dinners are the wonder of the nation!
With these he treats both commoners and quality,
Who praise, where'er they go, his hospitality."

" All human history attests
That happiness for man—the hungry sinner—
Since Eve ate apples, must depend on dinner."

———

ZANESVILLE, OHIO:

SULLIVAN & PARSONS, PRINTERS AND BINDERS, 87 MAIN STREET.

1876.

RICH WHITE SOUP.

MRS. J. FULTON.

Take a pair of large fat fowls and cut them up. Butter the soup pot and put in the pieces, with two pounds of the lean of veal cut in pieces. Season with one-half teaspoonful of salt, same of cayenne pepper and mace, cover with water and stew slowly for an hour, skimming it well. Then take out the breasts and wings of the fowls and chop the meat fine, leaving the rest stewing. Mix the chopped chicken with the grated crumbs of a quarter of a loaf of stale bread, having soaked the crumbs in a little warm milk. Have ready the yolks of four hard-boiled eggs, one dozen sweet almonds and six bitter ones, blanched and broken small. Mix eggs, almonds, chicken, and bread, pound well in a mortar, strain the soup from the meat and fowl, and stir this mixture in after it is reduced to two quarts. Boil separately one quart of cream or rich milk, and add it hot to the soup a little at a time, and let it simmer a few minutes longer.

RICH BROWN SOUP.

MRS. J. FULTON.

Take six pounds of lean fresh beef, cut from the bone. Stick over it four dozen cloves. Season it with one teaspoonful of salt, one teaspoonful of pepper, same of mace and nutmegs; (onions;) Pour on five quarts of water and stew slowly five or six hours, skimming well. When the meat is in shreds, strain it, and return the liquid to the pot, then add a tumbler and a half of claret or port wine. Simmer it slowly until dinner time or until reduced to three quarts.

CHICKEN SOUP.

Cut up two chickens, and put them in a pot with five quarts of cold water. Season with salt and pepper. Let them boil until the meat is very well done, and remove it from the liquor, and cut it up into small pieces. Put in the soup a quarter of a pound of butter mixed with a little flour, and a pint of cream. Throw in the cut meat, and just before you serve it add the beaten yolks of

FRIED OYTSERS.

Make a batter of the yellow of egg, flour, and a little water. Roll some cracker very fine, and after wiping the oysters, dip first into the batter, and then into the cracker. Fry them in half lard and half butter, till a rich brown.

SCALLOPED OYSTERS.

Fill a buttered dish with alternate layers of oysters and grated bread-crumbs, pepper, butter, and salt, (a piece of mace to each layer is an addition,) have a thick layer of crumbs on top. Place in a moderately heated oven, and bake fully an hour. When it commences to brown on top, place a paper over it, and allow to bake thoroughly through, then remove the paper, and brown to a rich color on top. No oyster liquor need be put in, as there will be enough when they are cooked.

OYSTER PIE.

Strain the liquor from the oysters, and put it on to boil with butter, and pepper, and a thickening of bread-crumbs and milk well beaten together, and after boiling a few minutes, throw in the oysters. Let them remain five minutes, take them off, and when warm add the beaten yolks of three eggs. Line a buttered dish with a paste, and fill with white paper or a clean napkin, to support a lid of paste, and bake it. When lightly browned, take off the lid, remove the napkin, pour in the oysters, set a few minutes in the oven, and send to table hot.

SPICED OYSTERS.

MRS. J. FULTON.

Pick over and wash the oysters, strain the liquor, and pour it over the oysters again. Then put over the fire with cloves, mace and pepper, and let them come to a boil, then skim them. When quite cool, add enough vinegar to suit your taste, and slice a lemon into it.

CHICKEN PUDDING.

MRS. C. PORTER.

Five eggs beaten very light, one pint of milk, one table-spoonful of butter, a little pepper and salt; put in flour sufficient to make a batter as thick as for pancakes; cut up a chicken, boil until tender, pick out the large bones, put it in a baking dish, pour over it the batter and bake until brown. You may add a few oysters if in season, and serve with the gravy the chicken was boiled in.

A Very Nice Way to Cook Chickens.

Cut the chicken up, put it in a pan and cover it with water; let it stew as usual, and when done make a thickening of cream, and flour, adding a piece of butter, pepper and salt. Have made and baked two short cakes, made as for pie crust, but rolled thin, and cut in small squares. This is much better than chicken pie, and more simple to make. Lay the crust on the dish, and pour the chicken and gravy over it while both are hot.

CHICKEN CROQUETTS.

MRS. HERRON, CINCINNATI.

Boil one large chicken, pick to pieces and chop fine; make a panada of three-quarters of a pound of light bread crumbs, a half pound of butter, and a little water; cook until the consistency of mush, and set away to cool. Add to the chicken, one nutmeg, pepper, and salt to taste, one teaspoonful chopped onion, one of parsley and a very little mace. Boil five eggs hard, rub the yolks and mix with the chicken, add the panada, mix well, and make out in shape of pears. Roll them in eggs beaten light, then in bread crumbs, and fry brown in hot lard, as you would fry doughnuts. You must have a pound of meat. Veal makes nice croquetts.

CHICKEN CROQUETTS. (No. 2.)

Take the white and dark meat of a nicely roasted or boiled chicken, (the former preferred as it contains the most nutriment,) chop it fine, and season highly with pepper and salt. Moisten it with a little of its own gravy, and form it into oval balls with the fingers, dip each one into an egg well beaten, and then roll in bread or cracker crumbs, and fry in boiling lard or butter. Serve on a hot platter, ornamenting the dish with slices of pickled beet, and sprig of parsley or celery leaves. A good way to shape cro-quetts is by using a wine or jelly glass.

OLD-FASHIONED POT-PIE.

MARTHA WELLS HALE.

Cut up one or two nice chickens, put into a deep pot, and boil until done. Then take some bread-dough, (a good time to make this is on baking day,) and after working in some shortening, just as if you were making ordinary light rolls. Make them out into rolls or dumplings, and set aside to rise. When the chicken is suf-ficiently done, make a rich gravy; about a half hour before you are ready to serve them, drop into the pot with your chicken and gravy your dumplings; cover tight, and do not lift the lid, *under any circumstances* until done. A half hour is sufficient to boil them. Serve immediately, for if allowed to stand they will fall.

BEEF, ALAMODE.

Procure a fine beefsteak, have it cut extra thick, then pound it well, season with salt and pepper; make a stuffing as you would for a turkey, spread it on the steak quite thick, then roll up and bind securely with tape, put it into a dripping-pan with water suffi-cient to cover it. Let it stew slowly for two or three hours, add boiling water if more water is needed. The gravy will require no thickening, but a glass of wine will improve it.

A Nice Breakfast Relish.

Chip some smoked beef, and drop into boiling water to soften. Let it lie ten minutes, and then put it into a skillet with a little boiling water, and stir gently for twenty minutes. Pour off the water, put in a little butter, and some pepper, and pour in a half tea-cup of cream five minutes before taking from the fire.

CHICKEN PIE.

MRS. NYE.

Line a pan with pastry, then fill with disjointed pieces of chicken, and strips or squares of dough; sprinkle with pepper and salt, sift in a very little flour, and add small pieces of butter; cover the top with pastry leaving a slit in the center; fill the pan with water, and let it bake an hour and a half. Just before serving fill the pan again with water. If the chicken is tough it should be boiled before putting in the pie, and the water used for the gravy.

BEEF BOUILLE.

Rub salt and pepper thoroughly into your beef, (the rump or brisket pieces are the best,) and steam it about five hours over water into which is put pepper, salt, sweet marjoram, summer savory, thyme, onions, carrots, two turnips cut fine, some parsley, celery and tomatoes if possible. When the meat is perfectly tender take it up; take out the carrots from the gravy, strain, thicken and boil. Pour over the meat just before placing it on the table.

ROLLED BEEFSTEAK.

AN OLD CINCINNATI HOUSEKEEPER.

Take a flank steak, wash and pound it well, chop one onion very fine and spread it over the steak, then sprinkle over it a teaspoonful of salt, a little red pepper, a teaspoonful of ground mace, a teaspoonful of ground allspice, a quarter of a teaspoonful of ground cloves and a half teaspoonful of nutmeg. Roll it up, and as you roll it sprinkle it with pepper, salt and a small quantity of spice, (the same you have been using,) tie firmly with a string; put it into a pot and just cover with water. Let it boil two hours, (keep it covered well with water,) until so soft that a fork will penetrate easily, then remove it from the pot, and set it where it will keep hot, and allow the gravy to stew down to a half pint. Thicken this with a small quantity of flour, add a small piece of butter, and pour this over the steak after it has been put on the dish for the table.

COLD SLAW. (Very Fine.)

Take a plate of cut cabbage, a teacupful of chopped celery, and a third of a tea-cup of grated horse-radish. Season with salt. Make a dressing as for lettuce, with the yolks of four eggs boiled hard, rubbed into a smooth paste, with oil, mustard, salt, pepper, and vinegar, stir this mixture into the cabbage a few moments before dinner.

SPINACH. ·

Pick it over and wash thoroughly, then boil in salt and water, pour over melted butter and vinegar, and sprinkle on some pepper, and serve either with poached eggs laid over the top, or with thinly sliced hard boiled eggs .

MACARONI.

Put the macaroni into a pot of boiling water, with a little salt in it, and let it cook ten minutes. Then pour on fresh hot water, and milk in equal quantities, and boil ten minutes more. Then put it into a deep dish, with alternate layers of butter, and grated cheese, until the dish is full, having macaroni on the top, with a little butter on it without cheese. Bake in an oven for half an hour.

STUFFED TOMATOES.

Scoop out the inside of a dozen large tomatoes, without spoiling their shape. Pass the inside through a sieve, and then mix it with grated bread-crumbs, salt, pepper, and any herbs you desire, or you may omit the herbs. Stew this about ten minutes, and then stuff the tomatoes with the mixture, tying a string round each to keep them in shape. Sprinkle them all over with fine bread-crumbs. Set them in a buttered dish, and bake them in an oven ; before serving take off the strings. Egg plant may be cooked in the same manner.

TO STEW TOMATOES.

Wash, and pour boiling water over them ; peel off the skins, and cut them up. Season with pepper, salt and butter, cook them in their own juice, half an hour. Thicken with bread-crumbs, and after ten minutes take them up.

CREAM CAKES.

One quart of sour cream, four eggs, one teaspoonful of saleratus, one teaspoonful of salt, flour sufficient for a stiff batter. Bake in muffin rings.

FLANNEL CAKES.

One coffee-cup of sour milk, two eggs beaten separately, and very light, flour sufficient to make a good batter ; just before baking add one teaspoonful of soda dissolved in a little water, also a little salt, add the whites of the eggs last. Bake on a hot griddle.

BROWN FLOUR MUSH.

Put two pints of boiling water in a kettle on the stove. Mix up a little of the brown meal in cold water as thick as you would to make starch ; then pour it into the boiling water, stir in dry meal until you have it about as thick as for ordinary mush. Then thin it again with boiling water, until about the consistency of starch, or as it was at the start, just let it come to a boil again, and pour into moulds, and eat as you would cracked wheat.

GEMS.

Into cold water stir Graham flour sufficient to make a batter a trifle thicker than that used for ordinary griddle cakes. Bake from one-half to three-quarters of an hour in a hot oven in small tin patty-pans two inches square and three-fourths of an inch deep.

DIAMONDS.

Pour boiling water on Graham flour, stirring rapidly until all the flour is wet. Too much stirring makes it tough. It should be about as thick as can be stirred easily with a strong iron spoon. Place the dough with plenty of flour upon a moulding board, and knead it for two or three minutes. Roll out one-half an inch thick and cut in small cakes or rolls. If a large quantity is required, roll about three-fourths of an inch and cut with a knife in diamond shape. Bake in a very hot oven forty-five minutes.

MINCE MEAT. (Extra.)

MRS. GRANT, PHILADELPHIA.

Five pounds of beef, two and a half of suet, five pounds of raisins, three pounds of currants, six pounds of chopped apples, one pound of citron, two and a half of sugar, four lemons, (juice and rind,) four oranges, one pint rose water, three nutmegs, two tablespoonfuls of ground cinnamon, one teaspoonful of cloves, one pint of wine, one pint of brandy. Add stewed apples and cider before baking.

MINCE MEAT.

Boil four pounds of beef and chop fine. Pick and chop three pounds of suet, wash two pounds of currants, and stone one pound of raisins, grate the peel of two lemons, and add the juice, an ounce of sliced citron, and twelve large apples chopped fine. Mix these ingredients with three pounds of sugar, half a pint of wine, and the same of brandy or cider, add nutmeg and mace to your taste. Bake this in puff paste with a lid on top.

APPLE CUSTARD PIE.

Take about one quart of stewed apples, one-half pound of sugar, small piece of butter; run through the colander. Then add the yolks of six eggs (well beaten), a little cinnamon and nutmeg.

POTATO PIE.

Boil one pound of potatoes, peel them, mash them through a colander. Stir to a cream three-quarters of a pound of sugar, and three-quarters of a pound of butter, add to this gradually a glass of wine, and one of brandy, a teaspoonful of powdered mace and cinnamon, one grated nutmeg, the juice and grated peel of one large lemon. Then beat six eggs very light, and add them by degrees to the mixture alternately with the potato.

PLUM PUDDING. (Baked.)

Into a quart of boiling milk put a sufficient quantity of grated bread-crumbs to make a tolerably thick batter. Let it stand until lukewarm, when it must be beaten well, and a half pound of butter, and the same quantity of sugar be stirred into it. Add eight eggs well beaten, half a pound of raisins, stoned, cut and floured, half a pound of currants, washed, and dried, and dredged with flour, a quarter of a pound of citron, sliced and floured, also a nutmeg ; a little brandy or wine may be added if preferred. Beat all well together, and pour into a buttered mould or dish, and bake slowly for two hours.

Make a sauce of three beaten eggs, a cup of sugar, and a gill of milk seasoned with lemon. Stir over the fire until it becomes as thick as cream, but do not let it boil, and add two wineglasses of brandy or sherry wine. This pudding may be boiled. Put it in a cloth which must be previously scalded and floured, lay it in a round-bottomed bowl while the mixture is being put in ; leave room for it to swell, and tie up very tightly. Drop into boiling water of which there must be enough to cover the pudding well, and replenish from the tea-kettle as it evaporates. Turn the pudding frequently. When it is done it should be dipped into a pan of cold water, to prevent it adhering to the cloth.

PLUM PUDDING.

MRS. J. QUETTING, BROOKLYN.

One cup of flour, one cup and a half of bread-crumbs, three quarters of a cup of raisins, three-quarters of a cup of currants, three-quarters of a cup of suet, one-half cup of molasses, one-half cup of sweet milk, one-half a teaspoonful of soda, one-half table-spoonful of cinnamon, one-half tablespoonful of cloves and a little salt. Mix well together, and boil four hours.

Wine Sauce.—Two eggs, one cup of sugar, one-half cup of butter, one cup of hot water. Brandy to the taste. Beat the whites of the eggs to a stiff froth and add last.

COCOANUT PUDDING.

MISS ADDIE WILLIAMS.

Grate the meat of half a cocoanut, stir it into a custard made of four eggs to a quart of milk, one tea-cup of sugar. Bake with an under-crust in a buttered dish, in a quick oven for thirty or forty minutes. To be served with the following sauce. One cup of butter, one cup of sugar stirred to a cream, then one cup of wine added slowly; set the bowl containing this into a vessel of hot water for half an hour, do not stir it.

ORANGE PIE.

MISS ADDIE WILLIAMS.

Three large oranges, eight eggs, two coffee-cups of sugar, two cups of cream, one-half cup of butter, three teaspoonfuls of corn starch. Bake as you would lemon pie.

WIGWAM. (A Nice Dessert.)

MISS COLLIER, PHILADELPHIA.

One pound of lady-fingers opened and spread on a dish; cover them with currant jelly, and on the jelly spread meringue, then another layer of lady-fingers, jelly and meringue; make several layers of the cake, jelly and meringue, making each layer a little smaller in order to have it pyramidal form; cover the whole with meringue and put it in the oven a few minutes to brown. The meringue is made of the whites of eggs with sugar beaten in, but do not make it too stiff.

LEMON CUSTARD.

MRS. NYE.

Six tablespoonfuls of sugar, two lemons, and six eggs. Beat the yolks of the eggs with the sugar, beat the whites to a stiff froth and add them, grate in the lemon peel, and squeeze in the juice, then add a small piece of butter, and bake like custard.

ENGLISH PUDDING.

MRS. H., OMAHA.

One cup of sweet milk, one cup of chopped suet, one cup of chopped raisins, one cup of molasses, three cups of flour, one teaspoonful of soda, one teaspoonful of cinnamon, one of cloves; steam in a floured bag four hours.

COCOANUT PIE.

MISS MILLS, OMAHA.

Scald one pint of cream or milk, stir into it while on the fire the beaten yolks of two eggs, and one cup of grated cocoanut; watch closely for fear it will curdle, add a little salt, and sugar to the taste. If the milk is not rich add a piece of butter. When baked spread icing over the top.

FLUMMERY.

MRS. H., OMAHA.

Take one cup of tart jelly, one cup of sugar, the white of one egg, beat the whole hard for fifteen minutes. Eat with cream.

ROLLY POOLY PUDDING.

MRS. H., OMAHA.

Make a paste of one-half tea-cup of butter, one quart of flour, two teaspoonfuls of yeast powder, and water sufficient to roll it out, roll it into a piece a half yard long and six inches wide, spread on it any kind of jam or stewed fruit, roll it up, wrap a cloth around it, and steam for two hours.

SAUCE.

One grated lemon, one cup of sugar, one-half cup of butter, one pint of boiling water, one teaspoonful of flour.

GINGER BREAD.

MRS. M.

One pint of N. O. molasses, one-quarter pound of butter, three eggs well beaten, one tablespoonful of soda or saleratus dissolved in one-half cup of warm water; make a batter like cake by stirring in flour to the proper consistency.

A New Treatment for Cancer.

Dr. Hasse, of Berlin, injects with a hyperdermic syringe, pure alcohol, to which one per cent. of ether is added, not into the new growth, but around its edges; thus obliterating he claims the vessels, especially lymphatics, which convey the infection, and causing the atrophy of the growth itself.

A Most Excellent Remedy for Toothache.

Alchohol one ounce, laudanum one drachm, chloroform five drachms, gum camphor one-half drachm, oil of cloves one-half drachm, sulph. ether two drachms, oil of lavender one drachm. Saturate a small piece of cotton, and put into the cavity; be careful not to touch any part of the mouth with it as it is very pungent; put the cotton on the point of some sharp instrument, put it into the cavity, and place a small piece of clean cotton over it.

CHOLERA MIXTURE.

Laudanum, tincture of Rhubarb, and spirits of camphor, equal parts. Begin with thirty drops, taken clear and unmixed, with a little sugar placed in the mouth afterwards. Repeat the dose (after every evacuation) increasing it if the case becomes urgent to sixty drops, (a teaspoonful), or ninety if necessary. No household should be without this remedy, particularly in the summer.

Another Mixture for Same.

Laudanum two ounces, spirits of camphor two ounces, essence of peppermint two ounces, Hoffman's anodyne two ounces, tincture of cayenne pepper two drachms, tincture of ginger one ounce. This is also invaluable. A teaspoonful in a little water, or a half a teaspoonful repeated in an hour afterward in a tablespoonful of brandy. This preparation will check diarrhea in ten minutes, and abate other premonitory symptoms of cholera immediately.

FOR SORE THROAT.

Take a small quantity of chlorate potassa, pour boiling water on it, and let it stand until it takes up all it will, then add old rye whisky equal to the amount of water you used. Add to this tincture of capsicum until the mixture is pretty sharp, and then it is ready for use. This is good for a gargle in all cases of sore-throat and is an excellent remedy for diphtheria, using it both as a gargle and internally. Dose.—One teaspoonful every hour, or when very bad every half hour. Water will only dissolve a certain quantity of potassa. A good rule, is to take a half a pint of water, and when it has absorbed all the potassa it will, pour the water off and add a half a pint of whisky. The capsicum is harmless so there is no danger of getting too much in, but to this quantity I should say add about two tablespoonfuls, which will make it sufficiently hot.

FOR NEURALGIA.

Alcohol one quart, sulphuric ether four ounces, chloroform two ounces, laudanum two ounces, oil of wintergreen one-half ounce, oil of lavender one-half ounce, camphor one-half ounce. Apply with a silk handkerchief. Half this quantity is enough to have mixed at one time, as the chloroform and ether evaporate so quickly.

Another Remedy for Same.

Bathe the parts affected every fifteen or twenty minutes with acetic acid No. 8.

MILK AS A REMEDY.

An article appeared lately in which it is stated on the authority of a very celebrated physician, that in the East warm milk is used to a great extent as a specific for diarrhea. A pint every four hours it is said will check the most violent diarrhea, incipient cholera, and dysentery. The milk should never be boiled, but only heated sufficiently to be agreeably warm, not too hot to drink. Milk which has been boiled is unfit for use. This writer says: "It has never failed in curing in six or twelve hours, and I have tried it at least fifty times. I also gave it to a dying man who had been subject to dysentery eight months, and it acted on him like a charm, he is still living, a hale, hearty man, and now nothing that may hereafter occur will ever shake his faith in hot milk."

CHICKEN SALAD.

Boil two (or if not very large, three) chickens; when cold remove all the meat from the bones, also the skin, and chop or cut rather fine. Wash and separate two large heads of celery, if celery cannot be procured, a good substitute is the nice tender part of a cabbage, with celery seed added to flavor it. For dressing, see salad dressing.

Updated Version

Ingredients:
2 cups chopped chicken; can use leftovers or rotisserie
1 cup plain yogurt
½ cup grapes, sliced
¼ cup walnuts
Pinch of salt
2 teaspoons curry powder

Directions:
Mix all the ingredients together and chill. Serve on lettuce or in sandwiches. If desired, you can substitute Old Bay seasoning for the curry powder.

Christianity in the Kitchen— A Physiological Cook Book

(1858)

This astounding book by "Mrs. Horace Mann" was published in 1858. Mrs. Mann, née Mary Tyler Peabody, was born in Cambridge, Massachusetts, in 1806, the daughter of Dr. Nathaniel Peabody and Elizabeth Palmer Peabody. Her sisters were Elizabeth Peabody, reformer, educator, and pioneer in establishing kindergarten, and Sophia Peabody Hawthorne, painter and wife of Nathaniel Hawthorne.

Mary worked closely with Horace Mann beginning in 1837, when he became the head of the Massachusetts Board of Education, became his second wife in 1843, and continued to work closely with him until his death in 1859. If Horace Mann was the father of American public education—there is a school named after him in most American cities—Mary Tyler Peabody Mann was its mother.

In addition to her work in education, Mary was a social reformer. She wrote *Christianity in the Kitchen* to serve as a moral guide to good eating. It was the housewife's duty, Mary believed, to educate herself in the latest scientific knowledge in order to keep her family healthy. Citing the research of scientists, she warned her readers against rich and fatty foods and advised moderation in spices and abstinence from alcohol.

In addition to *Christianity in the Kitchen,* Mary wrote a children's book, *The Flower People: Being an Account of the Flowers by Themselves;* many articles for various periodicals; a biography of her husband; and a novel, *Juanita: A Romance of Real Life in Cuba Fifty Years Ago.* She died in 1887 at age 80.

CHRISTIANITY IN THE KITCHEN.

A

PHYSIOLOGICAL COOK BOOK,

BY

Mann, Mary, Tyler, Peabody)

"MRS. HORACE MANN.

"There 's death in the pot." — 2 Kings, iv. 40.

"In that day, every pot in Jerusalem, and in Judah, should be holiness
unto the Lord of hosts." — Zechariah, xiv. 21.

Feb. 3

55

BOSTON:
TICKNOR AND FIELDS.
M DCCC LVIII.

BOILED BATTER PUDDING.

Eight eggs, eight spoonfuls of flour, one quart of milk; beat these together very thoroughly; put the mixture into a well floured cloth or a water rinsed mould, and boil one hour. Serve it with cold sauce. If more flour and less egg is used, boil it longer.

The same pudding may be baked in an oven three quarters of an hour.

BOILED BREAD PUDDING.

Pour a quart of boiled milk or cream upon a pound of grated or thinly shaved bread. Let it soak thus for an hour or two, and then mash it and mix it finely together; add four or five beaten eggs, two cups of sugar, a little lemon juice or essence of lemon, or a little mace powdered with fine sugar. Bake it two hours. Add raisins, or a flavor of wine for boiling, and let it boil four hours.

AN INNOCENT PLUM PUDDING.

Ten or a dozen soft crackers may be broken into a quart of good milk or cream. Let it stand thus all night, and in the morning rub the whole through a cullender. Add eight eggs, a pound of sugar, a cup of molasses, a cup of wine, a table-spoonful of salt, the grated rind of a lemon, half a teaspoonful of mace, a quarter of a pound of citron, a pound of currants, and a pound and a half of stoned raisins. Let it be boiled five hours, and served with cold sauce of braided sugar and butter and white of egg. Leave out the suet, cloves, nutmeg and brandy, that render plum pudding so deleterious.

SUNDERLAND PUDDING.

Make a batter as for a batter pudding, and bake it in small cups. Fill the cups two thirds full, having wet them previously with sweet cream.

RICE PLUM PUDDING.

Half a pound of rice, half a pound of raisins, half a teaspoonful of salt; tie it in a cloth, and boil it two hours and a half. To be eaten with sweet sauce.

BAKED RICE PUDDING.

Swell a large cup of rice, in milk or water, (milk being preferable,) add to it when swelled, a quart of milk, five eggs, two table-spoonfuls of brown sugar, or a cup of molasses, a little mace or cinnamon, a teaspoonful of salt, and a cup of rich cream; bake it an hour and a half. If the rice is put into cold milk unswelled, and baked immediately, bake it three hours. It will be a very good pudding with two eggs, or with the cup of cream left out. Raisins may be added if desired.

Sweeten three pints of cream or new milk, flavor it to the taste, add a paper of gelatine, and boil it thoroughly. Stirring it all the time, add the yolks of eight eggs, well beaten, strain it into moulds, and place it upon the ice for a few hours. Eat it with sugar and cream.

CALF'S FOOT BLANC-MANGE.

One quart of the stock, prepared as for jelly, one pint of cream, flavored to the taste, and half a pound of sugar. Let it boil up once, and strain it into the moulds through a gauze sieve. Cool it upon ice or in cold water.

RUSSIAN ISINGLASS BLANC-MANGE.

An ounce of isinglass soaked six hours in warm water, will thicken three pints of milk or cream, sweetened with half a pound of loaf sugar, flavored to the taste. It must not quite come to a boil. Strain it.

FARINA BLANC-MANGE.

Boil a quart of milk or cream, flavored and slightly salted; when it boils, sift in slowly four spoonfuls of the farina. Let the milk stand in a kettle of boiling water, and let the whole now remain over the fire an hour, otherwise it will taste uncooked. Pour it into a mould rinsed in cold water. Eat with sugar and cream.

DROPPED EGGS

Are more tender than eggs cooked in any other mode. Have a pan of boiling water ready, and break the eggs into a cup separately, and drop them into the water, carefully, that the yolk may not break. When the white is sufficiently cooked to be taken out whole, the egg is done enough. Dish them on toasted bread, dipped in hot water, and sprinkle on a little salt.

Eggs roasted half an hour in hot ashes are excellent.

KOL-CANNON.

The potato is deficient in gluten, and therefore not very nutritive. The cabbage is unusually rich in gluten. Boil the two, and the mixture is as healthful and nutritious as wheaten bread. Mash the potatoes and chop the cabbage, add salt and cream, or milk thickened with a little flour. Too much potato or rice renders people pot-bellied, but *kol-cannon* will remedy that effect of a too watery diet. The cream will add the requisite fat, which will correct the too constipating effect of the gluten, of which the cabbage contains thirty parts in a hundred, when the leaf is dried. Cauliflower contains sixty-four per cent., and would make a still more nutritive kol-cannon, which is an Irish dish.*

---

* See Dr. Johnston's Chemistry of Life.

FRICASSEED FOWL.

Cut a fowl into eight pieces, wash them, lay the pieces into a brazing-pan, or any covered stew-pan, pour on boiling water, season with a teaspoonful of salt, a bouquet of parsley and thyme, three or four cloves, and a blade of mace. Let it boil twenty minutes. Strain through a sieve, trim the pieces of fowl nicely, put half a pint of stock mixed with flour into the stew-pan, let it boil a few minutes, restore the pieces of fowl, add a gill of cream, mixed with the beaten yolks of two eggs, [called a *liaison* in French cookery,] and stir it quickly over the fire, but do not let it boil again. Serve in pyramidal form upon a hot dish, pouring the broth over the fowl. If any dish is to be warmed up again which contains a *liaison*, it should be done in a basin covered tightly, and set into a kettle of boiling water, else the sauce will be curdled. A glass of wine added, when the sauce is boiling, will improve the fricassee.

PEASE PUDDING.

Tie up a pint of split peas in a cloth, leaving them room to swell, but no more. Put them into cold water, and let them boil till tender; turn them out of the cloth, and rub them through a hair sieve. Add half a pint of cream, season with salt; mix all together with three yolks and one whole egg; flour a pudding cloth, place it in a small basin or bowl, pour in the mixture, tie it up and set the basin in a kettle of boiling water for an hour; when done, turn it from the cloth into a warm pudding-dish.

SNOW EGGS.

Flavor half a pint of milk and a little sugar with orange-flower or peach water, or any other essence; have ready the whites of six eggs, beaten to a stiff froth; (this may be done in warm weather in a basin that stands upon ice, or even in cold water;) add a little powdered sugar very gradually. While the milk is boiling, drop a table-spoonful of the egg at a time into it, endeavoring to keep the form of an egg; turn it over when fully set, take it out in a strainer and place it on a sieve, and arrange them in a crown on a dish; when all done, beat the yolks of four of the eggs in a stew-pan with a little sugar, and a few drops of orange-flower water or rose water, pour part of the boiling milk into it, to make a stiff custard, put it on the fire till it thickens, and pour it over the whites. Serve hot or cold.

CAULIFLOWER PURÉE.

Cleanse the cauliflowers, which should be small, thick, and firm, and let them lie an hour in salt and water, then rinse them in fresh water very thoroughly. Put them into boiling water, enough to cover them well, add two ounces of salt and a gill of cream. Put into a stew-pan a pint of soup stock, a turnip, and a little celery, cut up fine, then slice in the cauliflower, and when all is tender, mix in smoothly two table-spoonfuls of flour, two quarts of soup stock, and half a pint of milk. Stir it constantly until it boils, add one teasponful of salt and two of sugar, and rub it through a hair sieve. Restore it to the stew-pan, boil it five minutes, stirring it steadily and skimming it.

Throw toasted bread into the tureen when it is served, and stir in a gill of cream.

SPINACH.

Wash it in several waters, boil it ten minutes, or till tender, drain it on a sieve, pressing it with the hand, chop it up fine, put it into a stew-pan, with half a pint of cream, and a teaspoonful of salt, restore it to the fire in a little warm broth or soup stock, for a few minutes, and serve it hot.

BOILED RICE.

Throw a pound of good rice, well washed, into two quarts of boiling water; when well swelled, drain it on a sieve, put it into a basin or tin pail, and stand this into salted water that is boiling briskly, and let it stand until perfectly tender. Boiled thus, every grain will be separate.

PUFF PASTE.

A French cook puts the yolk of an egg and the juice of a lemon into the midst of a pound of dry flour upon the moulding-board, adds a pinch of salt, mixes it with cold water into a flexible paste, and dries it off with flour, using the hand as little as possible. Let it stand two minutes, and then spread half a pint of rich cream over it, fold it over from the edges, and roll it repeatedly, turning it often; lay it upon a floured baking sheet, and place it upon ice, if possible for half an hour, then roll it again. Cold water or ice are essential to this paste.

PAN-DOWDY.

Fill a dish with stewed apples, sweetened and flavored. Cover it with a good paste of dough that has been mixed with milk; when this is baked nearly enough, take it off and break it into the apple and replace it in the oven. If the whole has become somewhat dry, pour over it a teacup of rich cream.

Updated Version—Serves 8

Ingredients:

4 Granny Smith apples, peeled, cored, and sliced thin
½ cup sugar
½ teaspoon cinnamon
¼ teaspoon salt
¼ cup molasses

1/3 cup hot water
1 cup flour
1½ teaspoons baking powder
¼ teaspoon salt
5 tablespoons shortening
6 or more tablespoons milk

Directions—Preheat oven to 400 degrees. Butter a 9 inch glass pie pan and arrange the apple slices in the bottom. In a separate bowl, mix sugar, cinnamon, and salt, then distribute this mixture evenly over the apples. Bake for 20 minutes, or until apples are tender. While the apples are baking, sift flour, baking soda, and salt together. Cut in the shortening until crumbs start to form. Add the milk and mix until the dough becomes soft. When the apples are cooked, remove them from oven and add the dough to the top by forming small flat pieces with your hands. Keep your hands moist with water to keep the dough from sticking. Leave holes between the dough pieces for the steam to escape. Bake for 20 minutes, or until top is browned.

Putting It All Together

Gentle reader, now that you have mastered the intricacies of such wonderful dishes as shrimp wiggle, capilotade of turkey, and deviled brains, and solved the mysteries of "Mystery" (see page 96) and English Monkey (page 151), we thought you might be interested in learning how to put together a gala dinner. Toward that end, we present to you "Dinner Giving," from *The Woman's Favorite Cook Book* by Annie R. Gregory ("assisted by one thousand homekeepers"), published in 1902.

Good luck and good dining!

To the hospitably inclined, the pleasure afforded by entertaining those whose society is desired is unsurpassed, and nowhere does the host or hostess show to such advantage or disadvantage as at the dinner-table.

To give a dinner gracefully, however, requires tact; indeed, it may be said to be an art, to so select one's guests and so arrange them at the table that no lack of harmony will mar the occasion. The hostess must be, to a certain extent, acquainted with the peculiarities of each guest, and in placing them, she should carefully avoid seating two persons of opposite natures side by side.

She should study her guests, as it were; should allot the charming talker to the equally charming listener, and the opinionated person to the passive and yielding disposition. A dinner should be a function where no obstacles to ease and enjoyment exist. It is generally understood that all present are desirable persons and yet an acquaintanceship begun under such auspices need not extend beyond the occasion that gave it birth unless so desired.

Invitations to a dinner party are issued ten days or two weeks in advance of the event. The recipients of the invitation should reply at once, as to their ability to accept. This gives the hostess a chance to fill a possible vacancy. These invitations can be sent by post, but are better, because of more sure delivery, sent by messenger.

In giving a dinner an old saying should ever be kept in mind: "Good humor garnishes, good will beautifies, and good feeling gladdens more effectively than flowers, handsome china, or expensive silverware."

To-day a hostess of moderate means can invite fifty or even one hundred guests, for an informal party, without ever looking to the florist or the caterer for help, provided she herself is accomplished in that finest of fine arts—entertaining. She must, though, know how to bring people together, know how to group them diplomatically; how to bring out the harmonies of each nature; how to stimulate and inspire. If she can do this, then the results will be quite as satisfactory as though she had unlimited wealth and the command of all Christendom at her feet. It has been well said that the responsibility of the hostess is far less for the "warming, lighting, and feeding" of her guests than it is for the personal happiness of every one who crosses her doorstep.

ARRANGING THE TABLE

The first requisite for a well-ordered table is snowy, fine, damask linen. The napkins and table-cloth should be of good size and the dishes should shine with brightness. Underneath the cloth, padding should be laid. A table, when properly set, is a picture of loveliness—cut glass, silver, dainty dishes, with a background of white, appeal to the eye of the artist and why not to the guest, giving zest to the viands that are spread.

As to the manner of "setting" the table, there are some differences of opinion and greater differences of customs. At the strictest of houses, there are as many knives, forks and spoons placed at the different places as there are courses to be served. The knives lie on the right of the plate, and a row of forks on the left; the oyster fork on the outside. There are usually four forks and three knives; a steel knife for meat being one of them. The soup spoon lies next to the napkin. The napkin (which, by the way, should never be starched) is placed directly in front of each guest. Individual salt and pepper bottles are at hand, and if butter is needed, individual butter plates are called into use. A goblet is set at every plate.

A certain scheme of color is chosen, and everything on the table harmonizes with it. The flowers adorning the table are delicately scented and pleasant to all. There are many who dislike the heavily scented tuberoses and syringas, but roses, lilies, carnations, and lilacs are always agreeable. The dining-room is carpeted, or if the floor is hardwood, large rugs are used to deaden the foot-steps.

In lighting the table, lamps and gas are the most common method of illumination, but the preference is in favor of wax candles, as they afford good opportunity for decorative effects and make pretty shadows. The shades to the candles match in color the other decorations. In country places, the beautiful old lamps of odd designs with colored globes, are used, with fine effect.

The tables used are various—round, oval, or oblong. Many have large oval tops made which fit over extension tables, when an unusual number, like twenty or thirty, are invited. The advantage of an oval top is that one can get a better view of the company present and the *ensemble* as a whole.

DINNER TABLE NOVELTIES AND DECORATIONS

To the artistically inclined, an infinite variety of surprises in the way of table decorations is possible. The custom generally in vogue at the present time is flat center-pieces. If the table be oval, a pretty cut-glass bowl, filled with any low, sweet-scented flowers is in good taste, keeping ever in mind the fact that all colors should harmonize. Underneath the bowl, an oval, beveled-edge mirror or a round, fancy cut-glass mirror can be placed with good effect. Over the table-cloth, a few carelessly strewn rose petals, yellow and red, or red alone, are pretty and novel— these being appropriate only when roses are used as a center-piece.

The square table is more picturesque looking, when a square doily, either embroidered or of Battenberg lace, is placed in the center. For those who can afford the Battenberg table-cloth, nothing can be more exquisite. They are appropriate for oval, square, or extension tables. For a long table a Battenberg scarf, extending two-thirds the length of the table, is very rich and handsome. On one table, seating twenty or more persons, two or three floral pieces can be used, intertwined with smilax, with fine effect.

For receptions and weddings, medium-wide satin ribbons, pink, cream or blue, with or without smilax, fastened to the chandelier or attached to the ceiling and festooned to the four corners of the table, then looped and finished with bows of the same, are gay and charming in effect. The same colored satin ribbons, crossed at the center of the table and fastened at the corners, are also very effective; so, also, is one streamer of ribbon, diagonally crossing the table, with generous handsome bows at either point of attachment.

Ferns of all varieties are very handsome and appropriate, for either special occasions or for ordinary use. Smilax deeply festooned round the chandelier or suspended from the ceiling, reaching well to the table, is ever appropriate for public gatherings and suggestive of freshness, daintiness and beauty. Asparagus in its fragility, suspended in the same way and carried to the four corners of the room, and on it loosely hung fresh roses, pinks, jasmine or lilies, is a sweet bit of luxury. The same is true of autumn leaves strung on a thread lengthwise and hung fringe-like all around the sides of the room, not forgetting the table on which they should be securely fastened by a blind thread. These are most catchy.

I can conceive how beautiful the country dining-room may be made to appear in spring with a generous use of apple-blossoms, loosely twined and festooned, also made into garlands for the wall, reserving ever a generous supply of the latter, to crown the heads of the guests. Then again, in the fall, there are the pumpkin-vines, corn tied together by the husks, stems of luscious apples, all of which surpass anything made by art. Then there are the wax candles with the pretty colored shades and the lamps with the transparent globes that produce a sense of dreamland, to say nothing about those favored dining-rooms which permit of a good view of the brilliant sunsets of August and September. Subdued lights are always prettier than bright lights, especially so at the opening of the dinner.

Going back a moment to decorations, I believe the country homes are the ones most favored for display. My mind carries me back to girlhood and the Christmas times when grandmother invited all her children and grandchildren for a home gathering and how like fairy-land she made the festal board. The sweet-smelling spruce was brought into use, and everywhere were set these trees and branches, sparkling with crystals, converting the old-fashioned home into a veritable ice palace—a fit place for Santa Claus' reception. The secret she told us was this: The spruce was first dipped into a weak solution of glue, then rolled in crushed alum (not powdered). You who have never seen the effect, just try it once and see how like a million dew-drops in the sun it appears.

Then there was the china that sparkled and the glass that shone like jewels. Faded flowers she restored to freshness by first cutting the stems and putting them in very hot, then in very cold water; setting them in the cold storeroom till they were called into use. You would be surprised to see them come on the table, as fresh as though they had never been faded.

SERVING THE DINNER

In cities the usual hour for a dinner party is seven o'clock; in country places it is frequently earlier in the day. When the last guest has arrived, dinner is announced. The host leads the way with the lady whom he wishes to honor and the hostess comes last with the gentleman whom she wishes to honor.

The giving of a dinner is the most important of all the duties of a hostess. She must not betray ignorance or show nervousness, for she alone is responsible for its entire success. The serving-maid should be trained to keep cool and avoid accidents. The number invited and the outlay expended should depend upon circumstances and one's means.

The favorite form of serving a formal dinner is called *à la Russe*. The articles of food are carved by the servants at a side table or in the kitchen and brought to the guests. This has one advantage; it allows the host and hostess more time for social enjoyment with their guests. But it calls for well-trained servants to perform this duty satisfactorily. It requires about one servant to every six guests; therefore, when dinner is served in this fashion, where the help is inadequate, it is well to engage outside assistance.

For a home-like, informal, dinner, where the host does the carving, one servant can wait upon twelve persons and do it well if properly trained. On a table or sideboard should be placed the plates for the various courses, smaller spoons, finger-bowls, coffee-cups and saucers. As the plates from each course are removed, they should be taken to the kitchen.

The waiter should approach the guests from the left except in serving water, coffee, or anything of a like nature. The color and flavor of the various courses should be as different from each other as possible, offering all the foods in their respective seasons and of the finest quality.

COURSES FOR A FORMAL DINNER

First course: Oysters, as a rule, should be served at the beginning of a dinner, though they are used only in those months of the year in which the letter "r" occurs. The balance of the year little neck clams are used.

The *second course* consists of a soup, the clear soup being preferred, accompanied by crackers or bread. Celery may be served also.

The *third course* consists of fish, boiled or fried, and should be accompanied by small boiled potatoes; if broiled or cooked in any fancy manner, serve radishes.

Fourth course: An entrée is next in order if desired; it should be made in a fancy way, so as to avoid carving; bread should be the accompaniment. Relishes, such as olives, salted almonds, etc., are served with this course.

The *fifth course* consists of roasts. These may be composed of beef, veal, mutton, lamb, venison, turkey, duck, goose, or capon, accompanied by one or two vegetables.

Sixth course: Punch or sherbet may be dispensed with or not, as fancy dictates.

The *seventh course* consists of snipe, prairie-chicken, squabs, etc., but poultry, such as spring-chickens or duck, may be served instead.

Eighth course: Any appetizing salad with cheese wafers.

Ninth course: Hot and cold sweet dishes, consisting of puddings, ice creams, cakes, etc.

Tenth course: Fresh fruits and bonbons.

Last course: Turkish or black coffee served demi-tasse.

The above makes a pleasant menu, but it can be made simpler or more elaborate as one chooses.

Before serving the dessert all the dishes should be removed, save the drinking glasses, and all crumbs should be lifted from the cloth by means of the crumb knife and tray. A dessert plate and dessert spoon and knife, provided they are needed, should then be placed in front of each guest. Coffee (made after the manner of after-dinner coffee) should be passed last, demi-tasse, and served clear. Sugar and cream should follow, in order that those who prefer either or both may help themselves as they please.

TABLE ETIQUETTE

A host or hostess should never allude to the quality of the dishes or contents—either is in poor taste. The guests will discover their excellence without assistance.

If a guest does not care for a certain article, do not press it upon him.

Do not, in serving, overload the plates.

Do not finger knife, fork, dishes or anything on the table.

Do not overload the fork.

Do not leave the knife and fork crossed on the plate when you have finished, but leave them parallel on the plate, the tines of fork down, the knife to the right and the sharp edge next to the fork.

Do not, under any circumstances, put the knife in the mouth.

Do not drink from the saucer.

Do not rise from the chair to reach anything.

Do not tip the soup-plate or put the end of the soup-spoon in the mouth, except when eating oyster-soup.

Soup should be eaten from the side of the spoon and taken from the further side of the plate by moving the spoon from you.

Close the mouth when chewing.

Never make a hissing sound when eating soup.

Never cut bread, but break it, buttering each piece as it is eaten.

Never reach across others.

Bread should be buttered on the edge of the plate, never in mid-air.

Olives should be taken with the fingers.

The fork should be used for croquettes, patties, and most made dishes, and must be used equally well in either hand. Never eat anything with a spoon that can be eaten with a fork.

Do not hesitate to take the last piece.

Do not move the chair, but seat yourself quietly.

Look into, not over, the cup or glass when drinking.

Never quite fill the spoon; it is bad form.

A lady, if in a restaurant or hotel, rises when another stops to speak to her, even though she is seated at the table.

A gentleman half unfolds his napkin and places it over the left knee.

Do not mop the face with the napkin.

Napkins should be unfolded below the level of the table and as unobtrusively as possible.

Never tuck the napkin under the chin or in the waistcoat.

Soft cheese may be put on the cracker with a knife. Hard cheese is taken in the fingers.

If the host is carving, at a family table, it is not necessary to wait until all are served before beginning to eat.

The spoon is used for berries and cream, stewed fruit, peaches and cream, and soft desserts.

Crackers or bread should not be broken into the soup, but eaten from the fingers.

Strawberries served with the stem are eaten with the fingers.

The fork should be raised laterally and not in such a fashion as to bring it at right angles to the mouth.

The smaller knife, of two at the plate, should be used for fish. Never use a steel knife for fish.

Side dishes of vegetables should be placed at the left and eaten with a fork.

Never smear the meat with mustard or sauce of any kind; place it at the side.

Never transfer the fork from one hand to the other.

Never drink with the spoon in the cup.

Do not leave the spoon in the cup after stirring coffee or tea, but place it in the saucer.

Do not rest the elbow on the table.

The knife should be taken by the handle only, resting the forefinger on the upper part of the blade.

The fork should be used for mashing and eating potatoes. Never touch potato with a knife, except to butter it.

Ice cream may be eaten with either a spoon or ice-cream fork.

Pass anything which you see is desired, even to a stranger.

When through dinner, the napkin should be left unfolded, unless at home.

Ladies should always be served before gentlemen.

Never place toothpicks on the table and never use a toothpick at the table.

Never talk with the mouth full.

Never take a piece of bread with a fork.

Never put glasses on the table with the stems up.

Never blow on soup or coffee to cool it.

Never smack the lips.

Never leave the table with food in the mouth.

Never put salt on the table-cloth.

Always eat slowly.

Gentlemen should seat ladies first.

Do not bend over the plate for each mouthful.

Carry food to the mouth with an inward, not an outward, curve of the fork or spoon.

Do not spread the elbows in cutting meat.

Knives, forks and spoons should be placed on the table for all the courses except the dessert.

Finger-bowls are filled one-third full of tepid water, and are placed on the table only when fruit is eaten, and after a meal. The finger-tips only should be dipped in the finger-bowl.

The handles of the knife and fork should rest in the palms of the hands.

Do not tip up the glass or cup too much when drinking, but keep it at a slight angle.

Do not ask any one whether he wishes *more* potato, etc., but *some* potato.

Do not reach after a knife, fork, or spoon that is dropped, but ask for another.

Do not oblige the carver to make a selection for you when asked what part of the fowl you prefer, but answer promptly, giving your preference.

Do not eat onions or garlic unless intending to remain alone.

Do not eat after passing a plate for another to the carver, until the plate has been returned.

Do not twist the feet around the legs of the chair.

A crumb knife or fresh napkin should be used in brushing crumbs from the table.

Never shove dishes on the table; always pass them.

Never shove yourself from the table.

Never touch the face or head at the table or fuss with the hands.

Never suck an orange.

Never spit seeds of fruit on the plate, but take them out of the mouth with a spoon and lay them on the plate.

Never take a larger mouthful than will allow you to speak with ease.

Never hold the spoon so that the handle rests in the palm of the hand.

Never loll back in your chair or lean against the table, but sit upright.

Never make introductions after the guests are seated.

Never lift a glass by the rim; take goblets by the stem and tumblers near the bottom.

Never ask whether any one will have some meat, but whether he will have roast beef, beefsteak, or whatever kind of meat is served.

When asking for anything at the table mention, the party's name when you speak.

Do not give any one at the table the trouble of waiting upon you if there be a servant in the room.

Do not, when at a private table, leave until all have finished.

Gentlemen remaining for cigars rise when the ladies do, and remain standing until they have left the room.

Gentlemen allow the ladies to pass out first *en masse,* if all leave the dining-room.

Wear evening dress at a formal dinner party.

Wear gloves and do not take them off until seated at the table.

WHEW!

Glossary

À la mode or Alamode: When speaking of dessert, this means served with ice cream. When speaking of beef, it means braised with vegetables in wine.

Ambrosia: A fruit dessert made of oranges and shredded coconut and sometimes pineapple. In ancient Greek mythology, ambrosia is sometimes the food or drink of the Greek gods.

Apple Charlotte: A dessert consisting of a mold of sponge cake or bread, with apple filling, cream or custard, and topped with crumbs, baked and served hot.

Aperient: A mild laxative, either in the form of medicine or food.

Arrow-root: A gluten-free, powdery starch that comes from the roots of several tropical plants and was very popular in the Victorian era. It can be consumed in the form of biscuits, puddings, jellies, cakes, hot sauces, and also with beef tea, milk or veal broth.

Aspic Jelly: A transparent meat jelly made with stock.

Au Gratin: A dish baked with a topping of bread crumbs and cheese. The English word gratin comes from the French gratter, which means "to scrape" or "to grate," as of the scrapings of bread crumbs or cheese, and gratiné, from the transitive verb form of the word for crust or skin

Blade of mace: Mace is the bright red membrane that covers the nutmeg seed. After the membrane is removed and dried it becomes a yellow-orange color. When sold whole, it is called a "blade," but today it is normally sold ground. A blade would equal about a half a teaspoon.

Blanc-Mange or Blancmange: A sweet dessert commonly made with milk, cream, and sugar, sometimes thickened with gelatin or cornstarch, usually white in color. Set in a mold and served cold.

Bouille: Broth made from beef.

Boullion: A clear thin broth made typically by simmering beef or chicken in water with seasonings.

Breadfruit: A round starchy usually seedless fruit that resembles bread in color and texture when baked. The fruit comes from the tall tropical evergreen tree (*Artocarpus altilis*) of the mulberry family.

Brown Bread: A name given to breads made with significant amounts of whole grain flour and typically steamed in a can. The New England version probably came about because in the 17th century white flour was very expensive, so Puritans preferred the cheaper rye, wheat, or

192

corn flours. Few people had ovens at that time, so cooking was generally done over an open fire, making steaming a convenient way to make the bread.

Brown Betty: A traditional American dessert that consists of fruit, most commonly apples, baked between layers of buttered crumbs.

Calomel: A dense white or yellowish-white, odorless solid, the principal example of a mercury compound. It was used by doctors in America throughout the 18th century, and during the revolution, to make patients regurgitate and release their body from "impurities." Also called mercurous chloride.

Canapé: A cracker or a small, thin piece of bread or toast spread with cheese, meat, or relish and served as an appetizer.

Capilotade: A type of stew, typically of several types of meats.

Caudle: A warm drink consisting of wine or ale mixed with sugar, eggs, bread, and various spices, sometimes given a sick person.

Chafing Dish: A metal dish or pan mounted above a heating device and used to cook food or keep it warm at the table.

Charlotte Russe: A mold lined with sponge cake or bread, filled with Bavarian cream and sometimes decorated with whipped cream rosettes. Similar to an Apple Charlotte, only it is not baked and is served chilled or at room temperature.

Chartreuse: Game, fillets, etc., molded in jelly and surrounded by vegetables. Invented by the monks at the monastery of Chartreuse.

Chicken Marengo (also Chicken a la Marengo): Originally French dish created to celebrate the Napoleonic victory in the Battle of Marengo in June 1800.

Chow Chow: A pickled relish made from a combination of vegetables.

College Pudding: Baked or steamed suet pudding containing dried fruit and spice.

Consommé: A clear soup made of strained meat or vegetable stock, served hot or as a cold jelly.

Cream of Tartar: More technically known as potassium hydrogen tartrate, it is a fine white powder with many culinary applications. It is an acid and it is often used as a major component in baking powder, combined with baking soda to react when the mixture is moistened to ensure that baked goods will rise well.

Creole: Cooked with a spicy sauce containing tomatoes, onions, and peppers, often served with rice.

Croquette: A small cake of minced food, such as beef, poultry, vegetables, or fish, that is usually coated with bread crumbs and deep fried.

Croustade: A molded or hollowed bowl-like crust, made of pastry, rice or bread, used as a serving container for another food.

Crumpet: A thin flat cake, baked on a griddle.

Deviled: To prepare food with a spicy seasoning.

Drachm: A unit of weight formerly used by apothecaries, equivalent to 60 grains or one eighth of an ounce.

English Monkey: A dish made with a savory sauce of melted cheese and various other ingredients and served hot, usually on top of sliced, toasted bread. Also called "Welsh Rarebit."

Escalloped (or escaloped, or scalloped): To bake in a casserole with milk or a sauce and often with bread crumbs.

Eau Sucre: French for "sugar water."

Felon: An infection of the fingertip that causes an abscess.

Fricassee: Meat, fowl, or seafood, cut into small pieces and traditionally served in a thick white sauce.

Fritter: Fruit, vegetables, or meat that have been coated in a flour and egg mixture and fried.

Graham Flour: A whole wheat flour made by grinding the entire wheat berry, including the bran. It was named after Rev. Sylvester Graham (1794–1851), an American Presbyterian minister who was an early advocate for dietary reform. He believed that because white flour had nutrients removed and chemicals added, it was partly responsible for the poor health of Americans who had changes in their diets brought on by the American Revolution. Graham thought that using whole grains, combined with a strict vegetarian diet, would remedy these health problems as well as suppress carnal urges, which he believed were harmful to the body. There is some dispute as to whether Graham invented the crackers that bear his name, or if they came into being after his death. Some modern graham crackers are made mainly of the refined bleached flour to which the Reverend was opposed.

Gruel: A thin food made by boiling oatmeal or some other grain in water or milk.

Gumbo: A soup containing meat or shellfish and thickened with okra or filé (dried and ground sassafras leaves) that originated in southern Louisiana during the 18th century.

Hominy: Kernels of corn that have been soaked in a caustic solution (as of lye) and then washed to remove the hulls.

Kol-cannon, or Kolcannon: An Irish dish of mashed potatoes and cabbage, seasoned with butter.

Laudanum: Also known as Tincture of Opium, is an alcoholic herbal preparation containing approximately 10% powdered opium by weight. A potent narcotic by virtue of its high morphine concentration, laudanum was historically used to treat a variety of ailments, but its principal use was as an analgesic and cough suppressant. Until the early 20th century, laudanum was sold without a prescription and was a constituent of many patent medicines. Today, laudanum is strictly regulated and controlled throughout the world. [

Loaf Sugar: A large conical loaf of concentrated refined sugar.

Mangoes: When mangoes were first imported to the American colonies in the 17th century, they had to be pickled due to lack of refrigeration. Other fruits were also pickled and came to be called "mangoes", especially bell peppers, and by the 18th century, the word "mango" became a verb meaning "to pickle" (e.g., peach mangoes, tomato mangoes).

Meringue: A topping for pastry or pies made of a mixture of egg whites and sugar beaten until stiff and often baked until brown.

Mincemeat: A mixture of chopped dried fruit, distilled spirits and spices, and sometimes beef suet, beef, or venison. English recipes from the 15th, 16th, and 17th centuries describe a mixture of meat and fruit used as a pie filling and included vinegars and wines. By the 18th century, distilled spirits, frequently brandy, were being used instead.

Mock Turtle Soup: An English soup that was created in the mid-18th century as a cheaper imitation of green turtle soup. Often brains and organ meats were used to duplicate the texture and flavor of the turtle meat. In "Alice's Adventures in Wonderland," Lewis Carroll used this soup to name one of the characters, the joke being that Mock Turtle soup was made from Mock Turtles. Other "mock" recipes have been popular through the years, either through scarceness of ingredients or lack of money, such as Mock Oysters or Mock Apple Pie.

Mush: A thick porridge mad of cornmeal boiled in water or milk.

Mystery: A dish made from any kind of meat, chopped fine and then baked or fried, presumably a way to use up leftovers.

Newberg: Lobster Newberg is a dish reportedly created by Charles Ranhofer, a chef at Delmonico's restaurant in New York City in the second half of the 1800's. The dish uses a rich sauce of butter, cream, sherry, and egg yolks, and can be used with other seafood, such as Crab a la Newberg.

Othello Cake: A cake consisting of layers of vanilla and chocolate. It is named after Shakespeare's play and symbolizes the pairing of black and white.

Pan-dowdy: It is a deep-dish dessert that can be made with a variety of fruit, but is most commonly made with apples sweetened with molasses or brown sugar and a crust on top. The origin of the word is unknown.

Panada: A paste or gruel that is used as a binder. It is made from bread, flour, potatoes, or rice and used for finely ground meats or stuffings. The name derives from the French term panade, which means bread mash.

Parker House Roll: A bread roll made by flattening the center of a ball of dough with a rolling pin so that it becomes an oval shape and then folding the oval in half. They are made with milk and are generally quite buttery, soft, and slightly sweet with a crispy shell. They were invented at the Parker House Hotel in Boston, during the 1870s, and are still served there. There are several stories about how they were first created, but they all involve an angry pastry cook throwing unfinished rolls into the oven, which resulted in their dented appearance. The recipe for Parker House Rolls first started appearing in cookbooks in the 1880s.

Penoche: A fudge made with brown sugar, butter, milk and nuts.

Piquant: Having a pleasant, spicy taste.

Popover: A light puffed muffin with a hollow center.

Prairie Chicken: Either of two birds (*Tympanuchus cupido* or *T. pallidicinctus*) of the grouse family, found in western North America and having deep-chested bodies and mottled brownish plumage.

Pudding: A thick, sweet, soft and creamy food that is eaten cold, usually at the end of a meal. Today we use the term to describe desserts, but it started out as a description of savory dishes.

Receipt: An old form that means the same as recipe. Both derive from Latin recipere, to receive or take.

Rechauffe: A dish of food that has be reheated.

Rusk: A hard, dry biscuit or a twice-baked bread.

Sally Lunn: A type of enriched yeast bread associated with the city of Bath in the West Country of England, known since the late 18th Century. A building, now known as the Sally Lunn Eating House at 4 North Parade Passage (formerly Lilliput Alley), Bath, is a medieval building. It formed part of the Duke of Kingston's house in 1480 and was the first post office of Ralph Allen in 1725. It is now a Grade II listed building. The building was acquired in the 1930s by Marie Byng-Johnson who opened it as a tea-room specializing in Sally Lunn buns, promoted with a story that she had discovered an ancient document in a secret cupboard explaining that Mlle. Sally Lunn was a young French Huguenot refugee who brought the recipe to Bath around 1680.

Salpicon: A mince of poultry, ham, and other meats used for entrées, or it may be a mixture of fruits in a flavored syrup. Via French from Spanish, from salpicar, which means "sprinkle (with salt)."

Salsify: A root vegetable, also known as oyster plant because it tastes slightly of oysters. It has a beige-white skin and looks similar to a long carrot in shape.

Samp: Dried corn kernels that have been stamped and chopped until the coating around the kernel loosens and is removed. Can be used for porridge.

Scruple: A unit of weight formerly used by apothecaries, equivalent to 1.296 grams.

Shoofly, or Shoo Fly, Pie: A rich pie of Pennsylvania Dutch origin made of molasses or brown sugar, sprinkled with a crumbly mixture of flour, sugar, and butter. Supposedly it got its name because one would have to shoo away the flies attracted to the sweet filling.

Snipe: A long-billed marshland dweller, related to the sandpiper and woodcock. Recipes for snipe date hundreds of years, especially in Europe, where snipe is highly regarded and very popular.

Soufflé: A light, fluffy dish made with egg yolks and beaten egg whites combined with other ingredients and baked until its top rises.

Squab: A fledgling pigeon, about four weeks old.

Succotash: The name is derived from the Naragansett Indian word "msickquatash," meaning "boiled whole ear of corn." Today the dish is made with kernels of corn and shelled beans, especially lima beans, sometimes with the addition of peppers or zucchini.

Suet: The hard fatty tissues around the kidneys of cattle and sheep, used in cooking and also processed to yield tallow.

Sweetbreads: The paired thymus glands and pancreas of milk-fed veal or calves. The rounder pancreas gland near the heart is more prized than the tubular thymus throat gland. The pancreas gland has a more delicate flavor and smoother texture.

Syllabub: Milk or cream that is curdled with an acid beverage (as wine or cider) and often sweetened and served as a drink or topping or thickened with gelatin and served as a dessert.

Tapioca: A starch obtained from the root of the cassava plant, used for puddings and as a thickening agent. It can be made in flake, granular, pellet (pearl tapioca), or flour form.

Timbale (or Timball): A custard-like dish of cheese, chicken, fish, or vegetables baked in a drum-shaped pastry mold. Or, the pastry mold in which this food is baked.

Torte: A rich cake, usually multilayered, that is made with very little flour and lots of eggs.

Trifle: A dessert typically consisting of plain or sponge cake soaked in sherry, rum, or brandy and topped with layers of jam or jelly, custard, and whipped cream.

Welsh Rarebit: A dish made with a savory sauce of melted cheese and various other ingredients and served hot, usually on top of sliced, toasted bread. Also called "English Monkey."

Whortleberry: The edible black berry of a Eurasian shrub, *Vaccinium myrtillus,* of the heath family. They are found in very acidic, nutrient-poor soils throughout the temperate and subarctic regions of the world. They are closely related to North American wild and cultivated blueberries and huckleberries in the genus *Vaccinium.*

Dry/Weight Measurements

			Ounces	Pounds	Metric
1/16 teaspoon	=	a dash			
1/8 teaspoon or less	=	a pinch or 6 drops		.	.5 ml
1/4 teaspoon	=	15 drops			1 ml
1/2 teaspoon	=	30 drops			2 ml
1 teaspoon	=	1/3 tablespoon	1/6 ounce		5 ml
3 teaspoons	=	1 tablespoon	1/2 ounce		14 grams
1 tablespoon	=	3 teaspoons	1/2 ounce		14 grams

Dry/Weight Measurements

			Ounces	Pounds	Metric
2 tablespoons	=	1/8 cup	1 ounce		28 grams
4 tablespoons	=	1/4 cup	2 ounces		56.7 grams
5 tablespoons plus 1 teaspoon	=	1/3 cup	2.6 ounces		75.6 grams
8 tablespoons	=	1/2 cup	4 ounces	1/4 pound	113 grams
10 tablespoons plus 2 teaspoons	=	2/3 cup	5.2 ounces		151 grams
12 tablespoons	=	3/4 cup	6 ounces	.375 pound	170 grams
16 tablespoons	=	1 cup	8 ounces	.500 pound or 1/2 pound	225 grams
32 tablespoons	=	2 cups	16 ounces	1 pound	454 grams
64 tablespoons	=	4 cups or 1 quart	32 ounces	2 pounds	907 grams

Liquid or Volume Measurements

jigger or measure	1 1/2 or 1.5 fluid ounces		3 tablespoons	45 ml
1 cup	8 fluid ounces	1/2 pint	16 tablespoons	237 ml
2 cups	16 fluid ounces	1 pint	32 tablespoons	474 ml
4 cups	32 fluid ounces	1 quart	64 tablespoons	.946 ml
2 pints	32 fluid ounces	1 quart	4 cups	.964 liters
4 quarts	128 fluid ounces	1 gallon	16 cups	3.8 liters
8 quarts	256 fluid ounces or one peck	2 gallons	32 cups	7.5 liters
4 pecks	one bushel			
dash	less than 1/4 teaspoon			

Conversions For Ingredients Commonly Used In Baking

Ingredients	Ounces	Grams
1 cup all-purpose flour	5 ounces	142 grams
1 cup whole wheat flour	8 1/2 ounces	156 grams
1 cup granulated (white) sugar	7 ounces	198 grams
1 cup firmly-packed brown sugar (light or dark)	7 ounces	198 grams
1 cup powdered (confectioners') sugar	4 ounces	113 grams
1 cup cocoa powder	3 ounces	85 grams
Butter (salted or unsalted):		
4 tablespoons = 1/2 stick = 1/4 cup	2 ounces	57 grams
8 tablespoons = 1 stick = 1/2 cup	4 ounces	113 grams
16 tablespoons = 2 sticks = 1 cup	8 ounces	227 grams

Oven Temperatures

Fahrenheit	Celsius	Gas Mark (Imperial)	Description
225 degrees F.	105 degrees C.	1/3	very cool
250 degrees F.	120 degrees C.	1/2	
275 degrees F.	130 degrees C.	1	cool
300 degrees F.	150 degrees C.	2	
325 degrees F.	165 degrees C	3	very moderate
350 degrees F.	180 degrees C.	4	moderate
375 degrees F.	190 degrees C.	5	
400 degrees F.	200 degrees C.	6	moderately hot
425 degrees F.	220 degrees C.	7	hot
450 degrees F.	230 degrees C.	8	
475 degrees F.	245 degrees C.	9	very hot

www.ingramcontent.com/pod-product-compliance
Lightning Source LLC
Chambersburg PA
CBHW071529040426
42452CB00008B/939